"The idea of a crest-parallel trail came to me one day while herding my uncle's cattle in an immense unfenced alfalfa field near Fresno. It was 1884 and I was 14."

—Theodore S. Solomons,
"father" of the John Muir Trail

Fin Dome over Dollar Lake

GUIDE TO THE John Muir Trail

Thomas Winnett and Kathy Morey

WILDERNESS PRESS

BERKELEY

FIRST EDITION February 1978
Second Printing July 1979
Third printing August 1981
SECOND EDITION March 1984
Second printing June 1985
Third printing August 1986
Fourth printing April 1988
Fifth printing August 1989
Sixth printing February 1991
Seventh printing July 1992
Eighth printing May 1995
THIRD EDITION July 1998

Photos by the authors except as noted
Front-cover photo: Unicorn Peak and Tuolumne River, Yosemite Na-
tional Park, Copyright © 1998 by Ed Cooper
Design by Thomas Winnett and Kathy Morey
Cover design by Larry Van Dyke
Library of Congress Card Catalog Number 98-15796
International Standard Book Number 0-89997-221-7
Printed in the United States of America
Published by **Wilderness Press**
      2440 Bancroft Way
      Berkeley, CA 94704
      (800) 443-7227
      FAX (510) 548-1355

      Write, call, or FAX for free catalog
      Visit our Web site at www.wildernesspress.com!

Library of Congress Cataloging-in-Publication Data

Winnett, Thomas.
    Guide to the John Muir Trail / Thomas Winnett and Kathy Morey. – 3rd
    ed.
        p.   cm.
    Includes index.
    ISBN 0-89997-221-7
    1. Hiking–California–John Muir Trail–Guidebooks. 2. Backpacking–
    California–John Muir Trail–Guidebooks. 3. John Muir Trail (Calif.)–
    Guidebooks. I. Morey, Kathy. II. Title.
GV199.42.C22J637   1998
917.94'8–dc21   98-15796
                                                  CIP

Contents

Acknowledgments

If *John Muir* were alive, he would be at the head of the list of acknowledgments. Dead, he is still there. Muir's contagious love of the mountains afflicted all the early Sierra Club pioneers who conceived of a route from Mt. Whitney to Yosemite and inspired the building of the trail.

Among the living, my greatest debt is to *Jeffrey P. Schaffer*, who encouraged me to write the book, produced most of the maps and overlays, and himself mapped the trail from Rush Creek to Happy Isles. *Noëlle Imperatore* carefully drafted the rest of the map overlays. *Ben Schifrin* read the manuscript, contributing much from his fund of personal knowledge of the trail and of long-distance trekking. The late *Jim Jenkins* provided accurate mapping of the trail east of Crabtree Meadows. *Jason Winnett* accompanied me on the several trips needed to record a verbal description and photographs of the trail. *June Menda* turned my sketchy notes into exact and elegant profiles for the first two editions. Finally, *Penelope Hargrove* creatively put all the elements of finished type and art in their proper places ready for printing in the first two editions.

——*Thomas Winnett, Berkeley, California, April 1998*

Many people helped in great and small ways with my trail-scouting for and updating of this guide. I wish I had room to thank them all! In particular, alphabetically, I'm grateful to —

Polat Abdubek accompanied me, along with John Walter, on a ten-day leg from South Lake to the Sawmill Pass Trailhead. His unfailing good humor and accurate, strong throwing-arm were great assets to the journey!

Christopher Clarke, my predecessor in this job, whose draft rewrites were a valuable resource.

Rob Pilewski, the Crabtree Meadows summer ranger in 1997, freely offered information on the Whitney area, the latest backcountry weather report, and a cup of hot tea on an icy morning.

Bill Robens re-walked much of the John Muir Trail in 1997, partly in company with his wife, Kathryn, and happily shared his enthusiasm for the trail as well as his findings with me.

Rick Sanger, the Rae Lakes summer ranger in 1997 and author of the charming children's book *Are There Bears Here?*, generously shared with me his in-depth knowledge of the Rae Lakes and South Fork Woods Creek drainage.

Ed Schwartz, my husband, shuttled me between trailheads, supported me economically as well as psychologically, and put up with my long absences — though, I am happy to say, not cheerfully.

Michael J. Tollefson, Superintendent of Sequoia and Kings Canyon National Parks, supplied invaluable trail-mileage data.

John Walter and Nancy Peterson-Walter. John shared the same stretch of the Muir Trail with me that Polat did. John's skill as a backpacking chef deserves special mention. He can coax a maximum of nutrition and flavor out of a minimum of ingredients! Nancy shuttled the three of us from South Lake (Bishop Pass Trailhead) to the Sawmill Pass Trailhead — thanks!

Thomas Winnett not only gave me the opportunity to get into the guide-writing game but subsequently gave me the chance to update this guide, thus letting me, in effect, get paid for what I longed to do. *Such a deal!*

——*Kathy Morey, Mammoth Lakes, California, April 1998*

vi

Introduction

The John Muir Trail (hereinafter abbreviated "JMT") passes through what many backpackers agree is the finest mountain scenery in the United States. Some hikers may give first prize to some other place, but none will deny the great attractiveness of the High Sierra.

This is a land of 13,000-foot and 14,000-foot peaks, of soaring granite cliffs, of lakes literally by the thousands, of canyons 5000 feet deep. It is a land where man's trails touch only a tiny portion of the total area, so that by leaving the trail you can find utter solitude. It is a land uncrossed by road for 140 airline miles, from Sherman Pass in the south to Tioga Pass in the north. And perhaps best of all, it is a land blessed with the mildest, sunniest climate of any major mountain range in the world. Though rain does fall in the summer — and much snow in the winter — the rain seldom lasts more than an hour or two, and the sun is out and shining most of the hours that it is above the horizon.

Given these attractions, you might expect that quite a few people would want to enjoy them. And it is true that some hikers joke about traffic signs being needed on the JMT. But the land is so vast that if you do want to camp by yourself, you can. While following the trail in summer, you can't avoid passing quite a few people, but you can stop to talk or not, as you choose.

This book is your guide to this wonderful mountain world. It describes the JMT from its northern terminus at Happy Isles[1] to its *official* southern terminus atop Mt. Whitney and then to its *practical* southern terminus at Whitney Portal — nearly 220 miles of magnificent Sierra scenery. For those who prefer to walk south-to-north, this book also includes a complete description in that direction.

---

[1] Some sources regard Le Conte Memorial Lodge as a former northern terminus. All current sources declare the northern terminus to be at Happy Isles, at the base of Glacier Point. The confusion may arise from the Lodge's having originally been constructed at the base of Glacier Point in 1902–03, where it might very well have been considered the terminus. In 1919 the Lodge was moved west to its present location south of Housekeeping Camp so that Camp Curry — Curry Village — could expand.

1

The description and the maps are based on field work covering the entire trail. The maps are revised U.S. Geological Survey (USGS) topographic maps, corrected by Wilderness Press to show the situation as it exists. These maps incorporate more than 600 changes over the existing USGS maps, making them the most accurate maps of the JMT available anywhere. This book's maps are in a separate section in the book's center.

Planning your hike

The JMT is not a place to hike on impulse. Its length, its remoteness, and its great changes in altitude mean that you must plan your hike if you are going to enjoy it, or even to complete it. Before you can even do the planning, you need considerable experience backpacking in order to find out how your appetite behaves on long hikes, how much your body can take without rebelling and — particularly — how your emotions react in various backpacking situations. For example, you will have your own typical reactions to solitude (if you go alone), enforced togetherness (if you don't go alone), cold, hunger, and injury.

Once you know these things, you're ready to plan your JMT hike. To estimate how long it will take you, divide your typical day's mileage into 218.3 to get the number of days you will be hiking. Add the number of layover days you think you would like to take, and you have the total elapsed days. Then, using the mileage chart at the end of this chapter, you can figure just about where you will be every night if you stick to your schedule.

Hiking the JMT in "legs"

Or you may prefer to break your trip into several parts — one- or two-week legs — and spread it over more than one season. This book will help you do that: Appendix B lists accesses to the JMT and amenities found at or near those trailheads.

North to south, or south to north?

Gaining elevation, especially when you start at high altitudes, is more difficult than traveling mere miles, and the faster you gain elevation, the tougher it is. That's why, although the classic trip is south to north — Whitney Portal to Happy Isles — a majority of today's hikers prefer to hike north to south.

To begin at Whitney Portal is to start with the most brutal, continuous elevation gain of the trip — 5239 feet spread over 8.2 miles, up the east face of Mt. Whitney, from 8361-foot Whitney Portal to 13,600-foot Trail Crest — when you are least acclimated, least conditioned, and probably carrying the trip's heaviest load. This leg is typically spread over 2–3 days. Also, permits for Whitney Portal are extremely hard to get.

An alternate southern starting point, sometimes called "Whitney South," is at 9920-foot Horseshoe Meadow (see Appendix B). This leads to the Pacific Crest Trail (PCT), on which JMT hikers turn north. Two to three days' hiking (21 miles) brings you to a junction with the JMT just west of Mt. Whitney, near Crabtree Ranger Station. A couple of layover days in the area would allow you to dayhike to Mt. Whitney's summit. Permits for Horseshoe Meadow are easier to get than for Whitney Portal, and you don't have to carry a full pack over Mt. Whitney.

Starting at the northern end, in Yosemite Valley, the first major climb is rigorous but reasonable. You start over 4300 feet lower than Whitney Portal and the climb is more gradual — 5905 feet spread over 16.4 miles from 4035-foot Happy Isles to 9940 feet near Cathedral Pass, just south of Tuolumne Meadows' Cathedral Lakes Trailhead on State Route 120. The leg to 120 is usually done over 2–3 days.

Alternate northern starting points lie along a 2-mile stretch of State Route 120 in Tuolumne Meadows; see Appendix B, **Tuolumne Meadows.** Starting here cuts 2–3 days and over 23 miles off the trip, and your first day will be mostly a walk up *Lyell Canyon*, where the elevation gain is so gradual that the trail does not begin a serious climb until it is beyond Lyell Base Camp, at 9040 feet and 9.6 miles from the nearest access on 120 (Appendix B, **Backpackers' parking lot trailhead**).

When should you go?

Most of the JMT is above 9000 feet, where snows are deep and linger late. Unless you are experienced in snow travel, you'll want to go in mid-season, which, after a normal winter, is roughly mid-July to late August. Days will be warm but nights may be chilly, especially at higher altitudes. September days may be mild, but nights may be bitterly cold, and the first snowstorm typically dusts the range by mid-September, though it usually melts off.

After a dry winter, you may be able to enter the high country by late June; after a wet one, not before August. As you plan your trip, keep track of the Sierra snowpack so you'll have a good idea of the appropriate starting date to apply for. Agencies near the JMT usually have an idea of when the high country will open up; see the phone numbers and web sites listed at the end of this chapter under **General information sources.** Expect many streams to be cold, high, and swift earlier in the season; most streams aren't bridged. Expect to find snowbanks on the higher passes until August, maybe throughout the summer. Sturdy boots will help you kick steps in the snow, which usually softens by midday; a strong hiking stick or two will help steady you — and they're good for fording streams, too. Unless you have field experience in using an ice axe to arrest a fall on snow, an ice axe is probably more hazardous than helpful to you.

Sierra weather is typically dry, but afternoon thundershowers occur periodically, and it's possible to have several rainy days in a row. Be prepared for rain.

Supplies

Almost no one hikes the entire 218+-mile JMT without resupplying. If you hike very strenuously, you might average 17+ miles per day. Then you could finish in 13 days, if you hiked every day. If you need two pounds of food per day, and your non-food pack weights 30 pounds, you will start with 56 pounds, a fairly manageable pack.

However, hiking the JMT is the trip of a lifetime for many hikers, and they will miss a great deal by flying along at 17+ miles per day with no layovers.

Most people will average more like 8–12 miles per day, will take several layover days, and will therefore spread their trips over 20–30 days. Using the above assumptions, in order to complete the trip without resupplying, these people would need to start with a pack weighing 70 to 90 pounds, a daunting-to-impossible load, especially considering the elevation gains involved![2]

---

[2] Note that near the north end of the JMT, you can get supplies at a couple of nearly-enroute, seasonal, stores: Reds Meadow Resort Store and Tuolumne Meadows Store. More nearly halfway, but a few miles off the JMT, are the stores at Vermilion Valley Resort on Lake Edison and Florence Lake. See Appendix B for details of getting to/from these points. Except at Florence Lake, cafés near these stores can provide meals on the spot when open. However, the supplies available here aren't really suitable for backpackers; they're aimed more at anglers, day-trippers, and car-campers.

The best way to cut your pack's food load is to break your trip and walk off the JMT in order to resupply. You can resupply by mailing your food to a post office or package drop near the JMT, or by going out to a town to buy food suitable for backpackers.[3] See the end of Appendix B for details of sending resupply packages to post offices.

Going out to a town is practical only on the east side of the Sierra, and the best towns for resupplying are Mammoth Lakes (several junctions between 57.6 and 70.1 miles from Happy Isles, 148.2 and 160.7 miles from Whitney Portal) and Bishop (the better junction is 134.7 miles from Happy Isles, 83.6 miles from Whitney Portal). See Appendix B for details of getting to/from these and other towns/resupply opportunities.

Two seasonal resorts near the JMT at junctions roughly halfway along its length will, for a fee, act as package drops: you can mail them your food package, and they'll hold it for your arrival: Vermilion Valley Resort and Muir Trail Ranch. Somewhat farther away is Mono Hot Springs Resort, with a post office that can act as a package drop. See Appendix B for details of writing to them and of getting to/from them. *Be sure to write them well in advance to learn their fees and package-drop policies; include stamped, self-addressed envelopes for their replies!*

Wilderness permits

Appendix B lists practical access points to/from the JMT and identifies the agency from which you must get your permit in order to start there. Most of these trailheads have seasonal quotas; some or all of the permits may be reserved in advance. Unreserved permits, if any, are available on demand up to 24 hours in advance. It's a good idea to contact the agency from which you will get your permit well in advance in order to learn the latest details of its permit-issuing procedures, and to apply for your permit well in advance, too.

If you'll be starting from a Yosemite National Park trailhead, write or call Wilderness Reservations, P.O. Box 545, Yosemite, CA 95389, (209) 372-0740. Preference is given to ap-

---

[3] Caching food in the backcountry isn't practical any more; chances are your cached food would provide the local bears with an easy feast. Feeding the bears is punishable by stiff fines. The food storage lockers—"bear boxes"—found along the south part of the JMT are not available for caching food! They are reserved for the use of people currently camping in their vicinity.

plicants planning to hike the entire JMT in a single journey, which may include resupply stops. A permit is $3/person; make the check payable to the "Yosemite Association." See also _Mt. Whitney Zone Stamp_, below.

If you'll be starting from a Sierra National Forest trailhead, write or call Sierra National Forest Headquarters, 1600 Tollhouse Road, Clovis, CA 93611, (209) 297-0706, FAX (209) 294-4809, TTY (290) 322-0425. Permits are $3/person. See also _Mt. Whitney Zone Stamp_, below.

If you'll be starting from a trailhead in Kings Canyon or Sequoia National Park, write or call Wilderness Permit Reservations, Sequoia & Kings Canyon National Parks, Three Rivers, CA 93271, (209) 565-3708, FAX (209) 565-3797. Permits are free. See also _Mt. Whitney Zone Stamp_, below.

If you'll be starting from an Inyo National Forest trailhead, you can get a permit from Inyo National Forest Wilderness Reservation System (INFWRS), a concessioner, at P.O. Box 430, Big Pine, CA 93513, toll-free (888) 374-3773, FAX and TYY (760) 938-1137, 8 AM to 4:30 PM, 7 days a week. A permit is $3/person. See also _Mt. Whitney Zone Stamp_, below.

Mt. Whitney Zone Stamp. If your JMT journey will take you to the Mt. Whitney area, then no matter where you start, you must also apply for a Mt. Whitney Zone Stamp, which is $1/person. Include this cost in the check you write for the permit fee. Specify when you expect to be in the Mt. Whitney zone, which is roughly from Crabtree Ranger Station on the west to just below Outpost Camp (Bighorn Park) on the east. You must have this stamp on your permit when you are in the zone.

Animal problems

Wild animals

Experienced backpackers know better than to leave food and scented toiletries where rodents, birds, and bears can get at them. Besides protecting your food and toiletries — more on this below — avoid highly scented foods and scented/flavored toiletries. Check the hypoallergenic toiletries section for unscented products; use baking powder or baking soda instead of toothpaste. Rodents will chew their way into packs if the packs are tightly laced but unattended. Bears will perform near-miracles to get your goodies. As more and more people have taken up backpacking , there has been more and more unnatural food for bears — the food brought in by backpackers. Since this food is attractive to bears, and all too often easily available, the animals have developed a habit of seeking it and eating it. They patrol popular campsites nightly. As the bears have become more knowledgeable and persistent, backpackers have escalated their food-protecting methods. From merely putting it in one's pack by one's bed at night, and chasing away any bear that came, backcountry travelers switched to hanging the food over a branch of a tree. But bears can climb trees, and they can gnaw or scratch through the nylon line that you tie around a tree trunk. When they sever the line, the food hanging from the other end of the line of course falls to the ground. This happens all too often in Yosemite Park.

Counterbalance bearbagging, once considered a good way to safeguard your food, is now regarded as completely ineffective on most of the JMT — especially in Yosemite, Kings Canyon, and Sequoia national parks — and as no more than a delaying tactic on the rest of the trail. We'll describe the technique as we practice it below. Better ways to protect your food are using bear-resistant food canisters and using backcountry food storage lockers where they are available. Or you can camp well off-trail — but most hikers are reluctant to add the extra distance to an already-long day.

Bear-resistant food canisters are cylindrical lengths of strong plastic, sealed at one end and provided with a lid only humans can open at the other end. You carry the canister in your pack. A canister holds 4–8 days' worth of food for one person. They are widely available for rent or sale at outdoor stores and for rent at some ranger stations. On the north part of the JMT, you can plan your itinerary to match the capacity of your canister. On the south part, where resupply opportunities are more limited because of the long hikes out, you may combine a canister with the best job of counterbalance bearbagging you can possibly manage — and then cross your fingers. From Woods Creek Crossing, 165.4 miles from Happy Isles and 52.9 miles from Whitney Portal, south to Crabtree Ranger Station, you will have access to food storage lockers (below).

Food storage lockers (popularly called "bear boxes") are available at a number of sites in Sequoia and southern Kings Canyon national parks; see the trail-text for their current locations along the JMT. These large steel lockers have latches operable only by humans and are therefore considered bearproof when latched. However, some have holes through which mice, etc., can squeeze, so block any holes with rocks or sticks. Bear boxes are reserved exclusively for the use of people camping in the vicinity. You may not use them to cache food; you must not leave garbage in them. Never leave a bear box unlatched, much less open, even when there are people around. Rather, open it, put in or take out whatever you're after, and close and latch the box promptly. Word has it some bears have learned to hide near bear boxes, waiting for someone to open the box, upon which the bear charges out and tries to scare the person away. It's a bluff, so stand your ground, scream and yell to scare the bear away, and close and latch the box.

Counterbalance bearbagging. To counterbalance your food, use the following technique. First, tie a small stone to the end of a 30-foot length of nylon line (1/8″ or so in diameter) as a weight to hurl up and over a likely branch. The branch should be at least 16 feet up, and long enough that the line can rest securely at a point at least 6 feet from the tree trunk. When you have the line over the branch, tie a bag with half your food to one end of the line. Now pull it up to the branch. Then tie a second food bag to the other end of the line, as high as you can reach, and stuff any extra line into the mouth of the food bag. Now push up on the lower food bag with a long stick until they are equally high, at least 10 feet above the ground. If you can reach them standing on tiptoes, they are too low. Next morning, push up either bag until one descends enough that you can reach it.

REMEMBER: If a bear does get your food, it will then consider the food its property and will fight any attempts you make at retrieval. Don't try! Remember also never to leave your food unprotected even for a short while during the daytime. (In the absence of a bear box or canister, consider taking with you as much of your food as you can carry in your daypack, rather than leaving it counterbalanced, when you leave camp on a layover day.)

Pets

More than half the JMT's length is in national parks, on whose trails pets are prohibited. Leave your pets at home.

Summer rangers

To help you cope with difficulties and to see that hikers heed the rules for preserving the wilderness, a number of summer rangers are stationed along the trail in Sequoia and Kings Canyon national parks, and sometimes near Rush Creek Forks, from about July 4 to Labor Day. The trail descriptions below tell where they are.

Two points deserve special mention. First, if you go to a summer ranger station to report a friend in trouble and find the ranger out, please realize he or she might be gone for several days, so leave a note and walk out for help yourself. Second, remember that rangers have to buy their own food and camping gear, so they, not the government, are the losers if it is taken.

Stoves, campfires, and no-fire zones

We encourage the use of stoves instead of campfires in the backcountry. Using a stove conserves the finite wood supply for habitat and soil replenishment, reduces the risk of unnaturally caused forest fires, and doesn't add to the alarming number of filthy fire rings now defacing the backcountry.

Along the JMT, wood fires are prohibited above 9600 feet in Yosemite; above 10,000 feet in the drainage of the Kings and San Joaquin rivers in Kings Canyon National Park; and above 11,200 feet in Sequoia National Park. In addition, in Sequoia, wood fires are prohibited within 1200 feet of Tyndall Creek crossing and of Tyndall Creek frogponds (Tyndall Frog Ponds), and above 10,800 feet in the Wallace and Wright Creek drainages.

Be sure to study and take with you for reference the information you get with your permit(s) on the latest fire and camping regulations!

Going lighter

For ideas on lightening your load, check out Ray Jardine's *The Pacific Crest Trail Hiker's Handbook*, 2nd ed., AdventureLore Press, La Pine, OR, 1996 (also available through Wilderness Press). We don't agree with all it says, but it's definitely enlightening — pun intended!

General information sources

The JMT passes through Yosemite, Kings Canyon, and

Sequoia national parks and through Sierra and Inyo National Forests. For general information from those agencies:

- Yosemite National Park, (209) 372-0200 (press option 5 for wilderness information), www.nps.gov/yose
- Kings Canyon-Sequoia National Parks, (209) 565-3341 (headquarters), www.nps.gov/seki
- Sierra National Forest, (209) 297-0706 (headquarters), www.r5.pswfs.gov/sierra/ (site may not yet be fully operational)
- Inyo National Forest, (760) 873-2400 (headquarters), www.r5.pswfs.gov/inyo/index.htm

GORP, the Great Outdoors Recreation Pages, at www.gorp.com is another good source of general information.

Topographic Trail Maps
for the
John Muir Trail

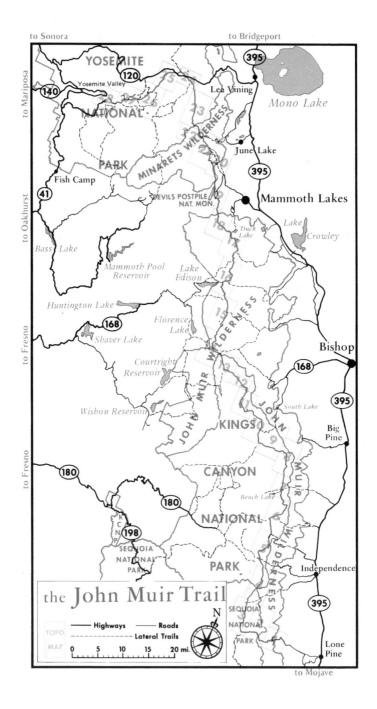

the **John Muir Trail**

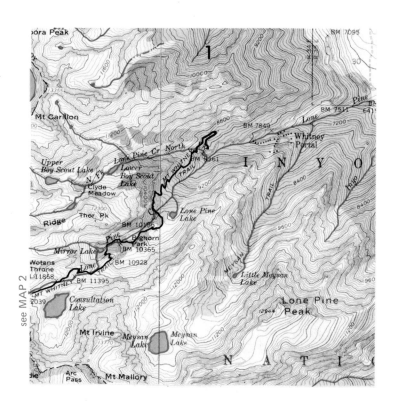

see MAP 2

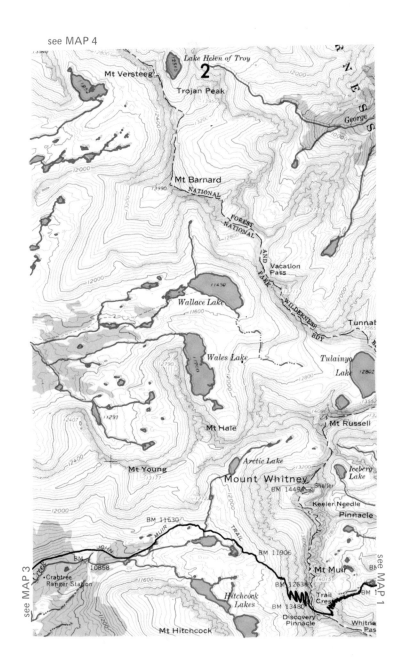

see MAP 3

see MAP 1

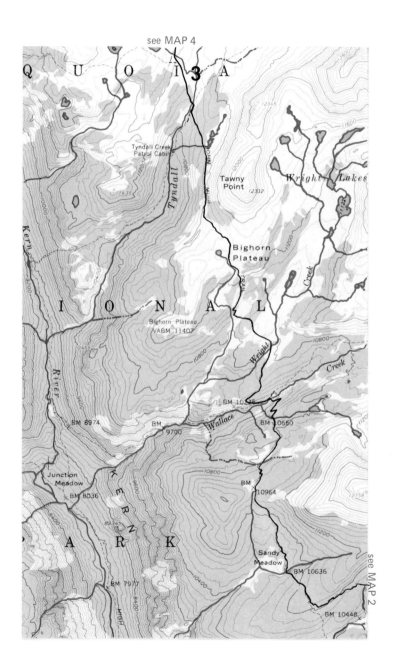

Q U O I 3 A

Tyndall Creek
Patrol Cabin

Tyndall

Tawny
Point
12332

Wright Lakes

Bighorn
Plateau

Kern

I O N A L

Bighorn Plateau
VABM 11402

Wright

Creek

TRAIL

Wright

Creek

River

BM 10325

BM 8974

BM
9700

Wallace

BM 10650

Junction
Meadow

BM 8036

K E R N

BM
10964

8934

P A R K

Sandy
Meadow

BM 10636

BM 7977

BM 10448

see MAP 2

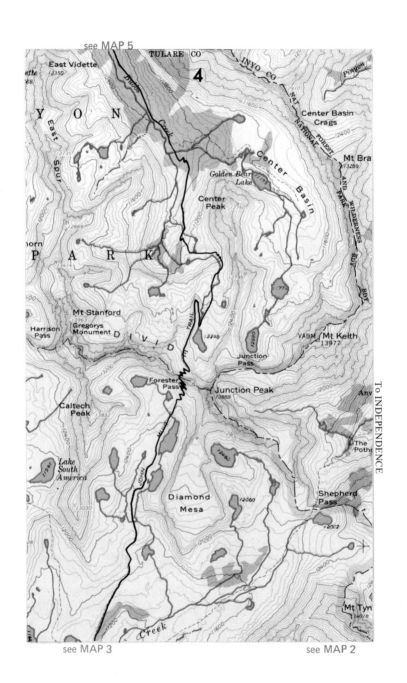

see MAP 5

TULARE CO

4

East Vidette
12350

INYO CO

Pinyon

NATIONAL

Center Basin
Crags

12400

Mt Bra
13289

Center Basin

Golden Bear
Lake

Center
Peak

N O Y

East Spur

2735

2889

FOREST

AND PARK WILDERNESS BDY

BDY

P A R K

141

Mt Stanford
13963
Gregorys
Monument

Harrison
Pass

12248

VABM / Mt Keith
13977

norn

D I V I D

Junction
Pass

To INDEPENDENCE

Forester Pass

Junction Peak
13888

Caltech
Peak *13832*

Anv

The Poth

Lake
South
America

3030

JOHN

Diamond
Mesa

12060

Shepherd Pass

12002

11931

Mt Tyn
14018

Creek

see MAP 3   see MAP 2

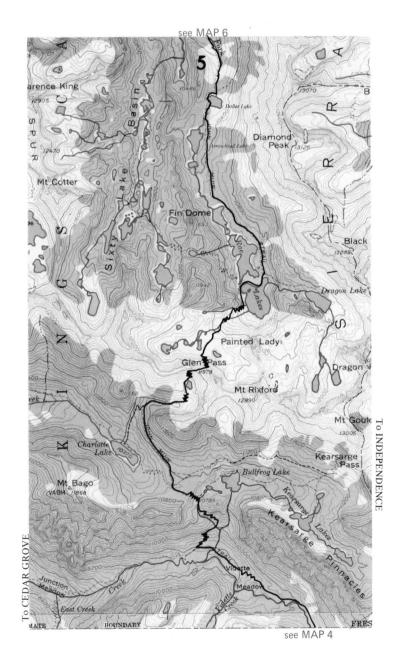

see MAP 6

5

To CEDAR GROVE

To INDEPENDENCE

see MAP 4

Clarence King
12905

SPUR

12470

Mt Cotter

Sixty Lake Basin

Lake

Fin Dome
11693

KINGS

11553

11942

11200

Glen Pass
11978

9568

Charlotte Lake
10271

Mt Bago
VABM 11868

Junction Meadow

East Creek

Creek

Dollar Lake

Arrowhead Lake

13070

Diamond Peak
13126

Black
13289

Dragon Lake

Painted Lady
12126

Mt Rixford
12890

Dragon

Mt Goul
13005

Kearsarge Pass

Bullfrog Lake

Charlotte Creek

Kearsarge Lakes

Kearsarge Pinnacles

Vidette Meadow

Vidette Creek

SIERRA

B

ULTIMATE BOUNDARY

FRES

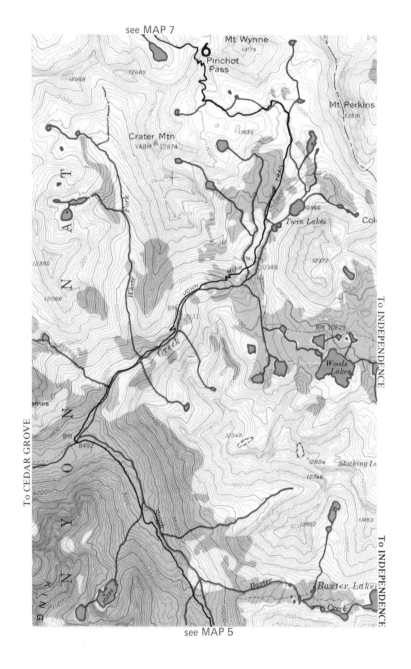

see MAP 7

Mt Wynne
13179

6 Pinchot Pass

Mt Perkins
12591

12685

12968

12000

11635

Crater Mtn
VABM *12874*

12000

12350

12068

White Fork

JOHN

MUIR

TRAIL

Twin Lakes
10966

Col

12372

10346

BM *9531*

BM 10829

Woods Lake

Creek

10400

12349

12804 Stocking L

12746

11600

12852

13183

ames

BM *8492*

9200

9000

South

Baxter

Baxter Lake

Creek

see MAP 5

To CEDAR GROVE

To INDEPENDENCE

To INDEPENDENCE

KINGS
CANYON

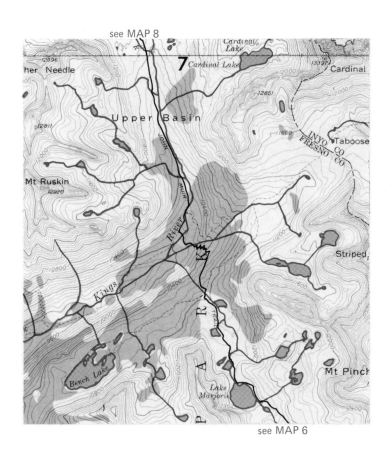

7

Cardinal Lake

Cardinal Lake

her Needle

Cardinal

Upper Basin

Taboose

INYO CO.
FRESNO CO.

Mt Ruskin

Striped

Kings River

Bench Lake

Lake Marjorie

Mt Pinch

see MAP 6

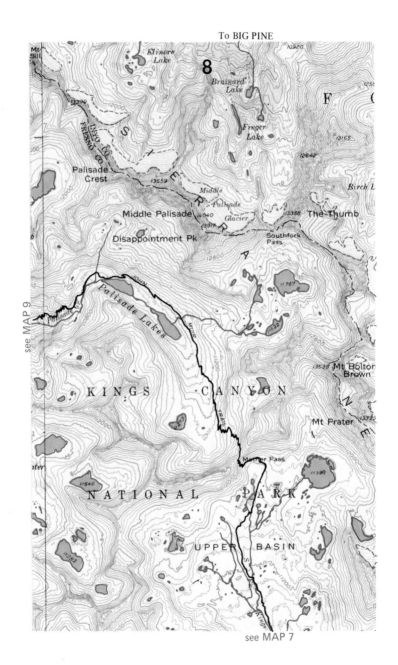

8

Elinore
Lake

Brainard
Lake

Finger
Lake

Palisade
Crest

Middle
Palisade

Middle Palisade
Glacier

The Thumb

Disappointment Pk

Southfork
Pass

see MAP 9

Palisade Lakes

Mt Bolton
Brown

KINGS   CANYON

Mt Prater

Mather Pass

NATIONAL   PARK

UPPER   BASIN

see MAP 7

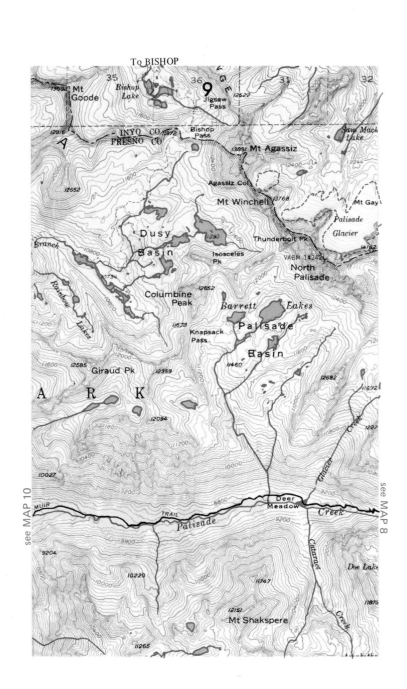

35   36   **9**   31   32

13082   Mt
Goode

Bishop
Lake

11600

Jigsaw
Pass

12622

12916   INYO CO   11372
FRESNO CO

Bishop
Pass

Sam Mack
Lake

12652

13891   Mt Agassiz

12400

12400

11244

11600

Agassiz Col

Mt Winchell   13768

Mt Gay

D u s y

11393

Thunderbolt Pk

Palisade
Glacier

14162

B a s i n

Isosceles
Pk

12000

VABM 14242

North
Palisade

11574

12400

Branch

10800

Columbine
Peak

12652

Rosenbow

11200

11673

Barrett   Eakes

P a l i s a d e

Lakes

Knapsack
Pass

B a s i n

11600

11200

11460

12692

12585   11600

Giraud Pk   12359

11200

11372

A   R   K

12094

11600

10800

Glacier Creek

11222

11200

10400

10000

10000

9200

10027

8800

Deer
Meadow

Creek

9200

9200

Palisade

MUIR   TRAIL

8800

9204

8800

Cataract Creek

Doe Lake

10220

10000

10000

11747

11875

10000

12151

Mt Shakspere

11265

see MAP 10

see MAP 8

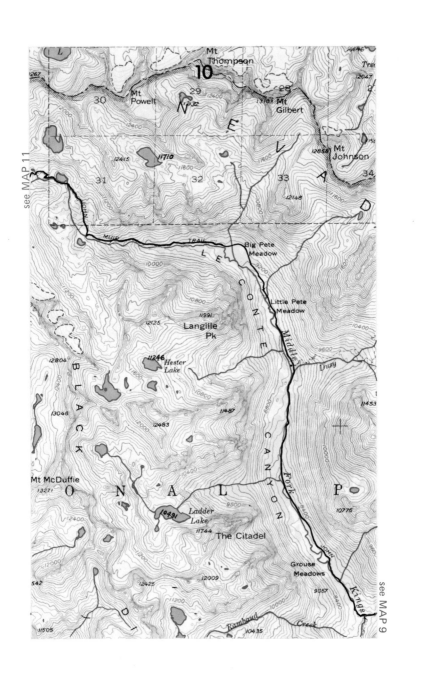

see MAP 11

see MAP 9

Mt
Thompson

10

Mt
Powell

Mt
Gilbert

Mt
Johnson

Big Pete
Meadow

Little Pete
Meadow

Langille
Pk

Hester
Lake

Mt McDuffie

Ladder
Lake

The Citadel

Grouse
Meadows

Rambaud   Creek

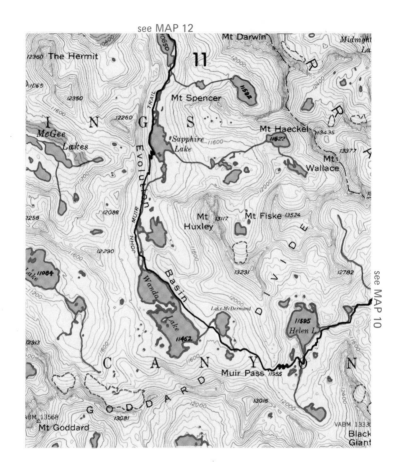

see MAP 10

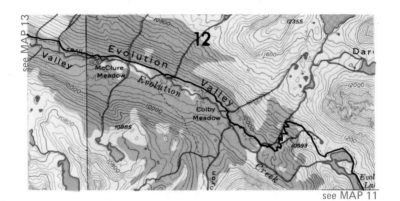

see MAP 13

12

see MAP 11

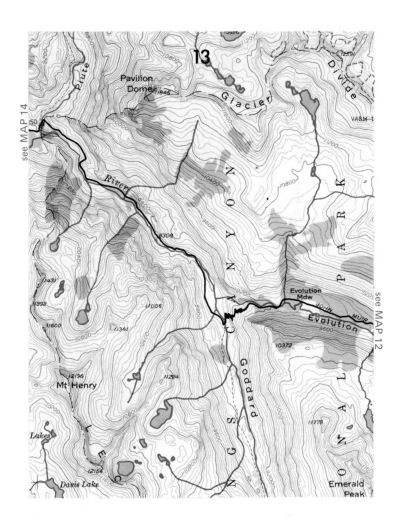

see MAP 14

see MAP 12

Piute

Pavilion
Dome *11946*

Glacier

Divide

12591

VABM 1

9850

River

N

Y

O

N

A

C

8308

Evolution
Mdw

JOHN

MUIR

PARK

Evolution

9600

10372

1143I

11392

11600

11006

11341

9800

Goddard

N

O

11778

12196

Mt Henry

11224

Lakes

12154

Davis Lake

V

A

L

L

E

Y

Emerald
Peak

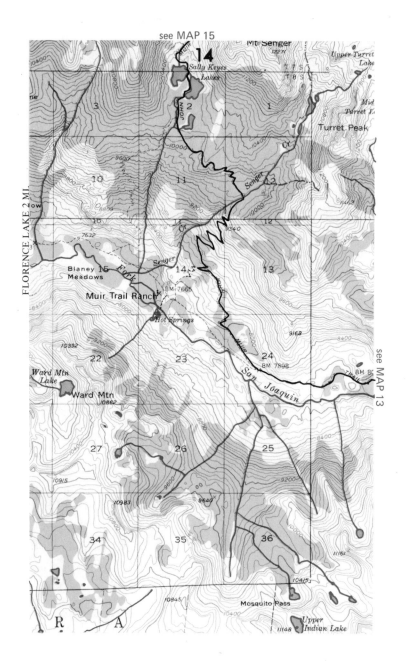

see MAP 13

see MAP 16

15

Kip Camp

A T I O N A L

Bear

Creek

Higgins

Cergile

Bear Twin
Lakes

Marcella
Lake

Creek

Cirque
Lake

Apollo Lake

Depressed
Lake

F O R E S T

Orchid
Lake

Rosemarie
Meadow

Lou Beverly
Lake

East

West Fork

South

Creek

Rosebud
Lake

Rose Lake

Lake

Harvey
Lake

Foolish Lake

Hooper
Lake

Crazy
Lake

Marshall
Lake

Marie
Lake

Medle

Neil Lake

Flat Note
Lake

Mt Hooper
VABM 12349

Chamberlain
Lake

Selden Pass

Sharp N
Lake

Heart
Lake

see MAP 14

see MAP 17

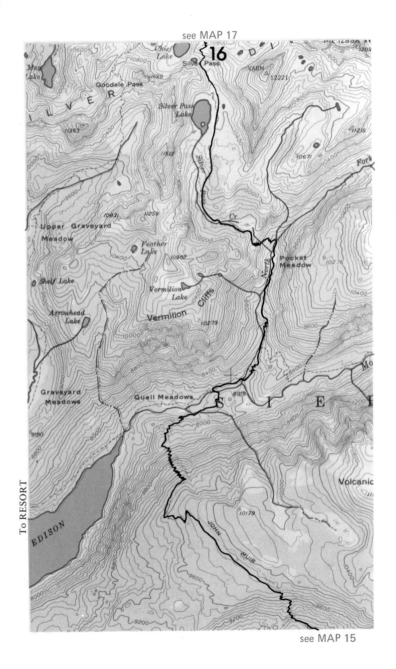

see MAP 15

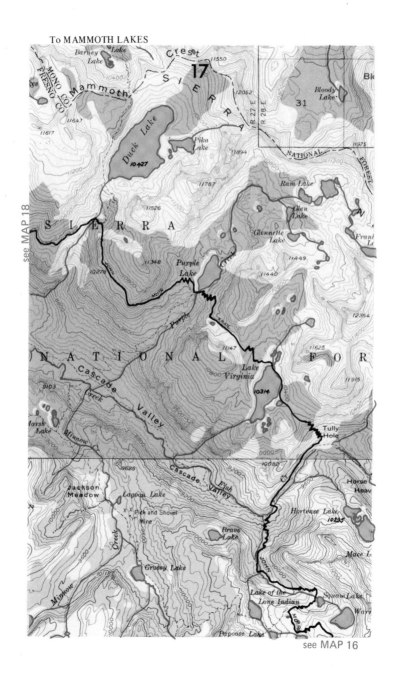

see MAP 18

see MAP 16

see MAP 19

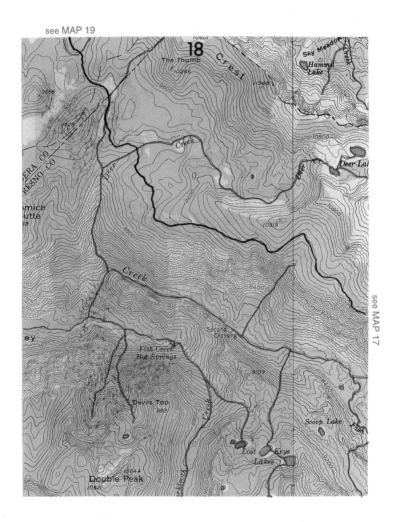

see MAP 17

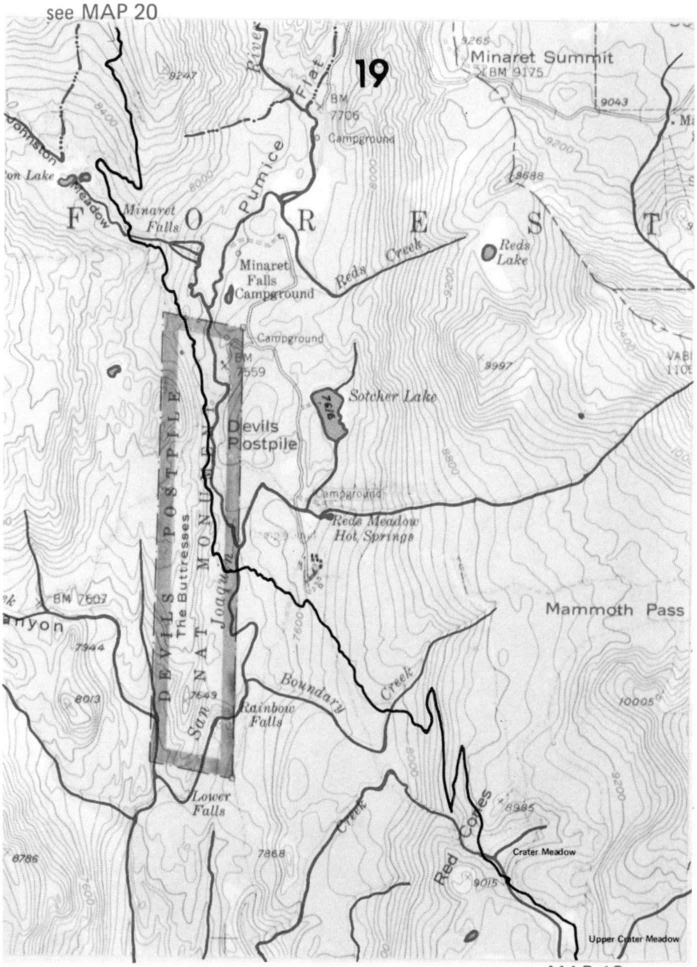

19

Minaret Summit
BM 9175

To MAMMOTH LAKES

9247

9043

BM
7706
Campground

9666

Mi

3688

F   O   R   E   S   T

Johnston Lake

Freedom

Minaret
Falls

8000

Pumice   Flat

Reds   Creek

Reds
Lake

Minaret
Falls
Campground

9200

Campground

8997

BM
7559

Sotcher Lake

7618

9000

Devils
Postpile

Campground

DEVILS   POSTPILE

Reds Meadow
Hot Springs

To MAMMOTH LAKES

The Buttresses

BM 7607

Canyon

7944

8013

7649

San   Joaquin   NAT   MONUME

7500

Mammoth Pass

Boundary   Creek

Rainbow
Falls

10005

Lower
Falls

8786

7868

8000

Red   Cones

8995

9015

Crater Meadow

Upper Crater Meadow

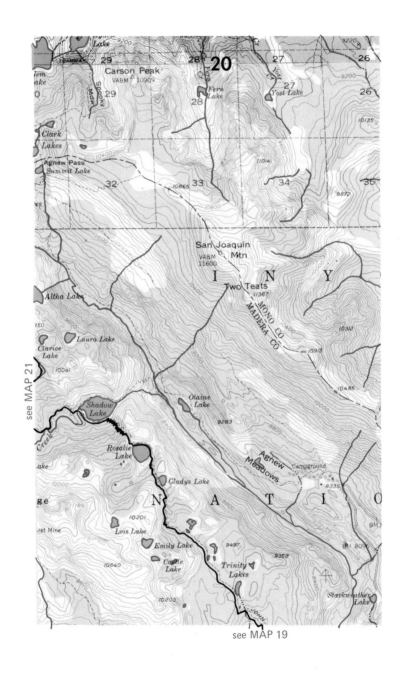

Lake

TRAMWAY 29

Carson Peak
VABM 10909

29

28

27

26

Fern
Lake

28

Yost
Lake

27

26

Clark
Lakes

Agnew Pass
Summit Lake

32

33

34

35

San Joaquin
Mtn
VABM
11600

I N Y

Two Teats

Altha Lake

MONO CO.
MADERA CO.

Laura Lake

Clarice
Lake

Shadow
Lake

Olaine
Lake

Agnew
Meadows

Campground

Rosalie
Lake

Creek

Gladys Lake

N

A

T

I

O

Lois Lake

ret Mine

Emily Lake

Castle
Lake

Trinity
Lakes

Starkweather
Lake

see MAP 21

see MAP 19

see MAP 22

To JUNE LAKE

see MAP 20

19

30

31

10253

10365

8052

Gem Lake

Billy Lake

Waugh Lake
9424

Rush Cr.

Rush Cr.

Rush Creek

Waugh Lake

9600

10181

Weber Lake
10508

Sullivan Lake

Island Pass

10492

10587

10474

Thousand Island Lake

JOHN

Emerald Lake

Badger Lake

lakes

8834

Ruby Lake

10365

11501

Davis

10572

10000

Garnet Lake

10324

10000

Lake Catherine

11158

1034

10736

Banner Peak
12945

10704

Nydiver Lakes

10800

Mt Ritter
13157

9600

Shadow

Ediza Lake

Cabin

12344

Volcanic Ridge
11241

Iceberg Lake

11501

1204

10287

10000

see MAP 23

see MAP 21

22

Mt Maclure

Cathedral

Lyell

TUOLUMNE

Range

Glacier

INYO

CO.

NATIONAL

Marie Lakes

Mt Lyell

VABM 13114

MONO CO.

MADERA CO.

FOREST

Marie
Lakes

Rodgers
Lakes

Rodgers PK

12978

MONO CO.
MADERA CO.

12037

11627

Davis
Lake

Mt C

R

see MAP 24

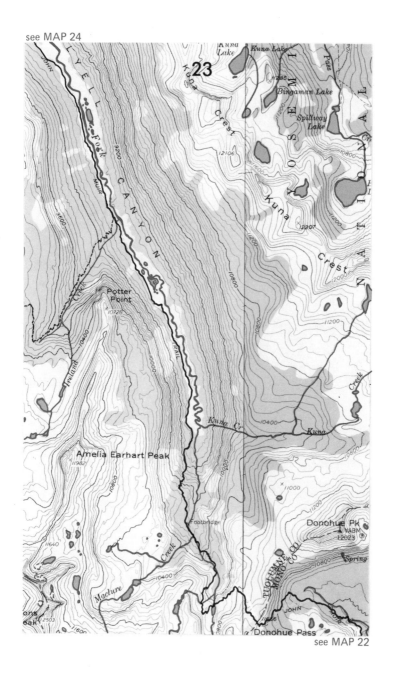

see MAP 22

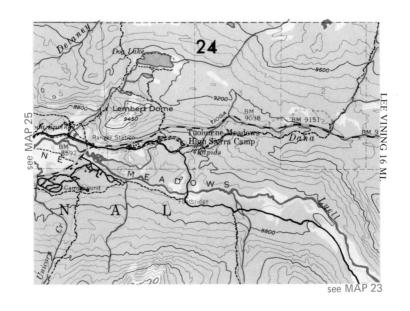

see MAP 25

LEE VINING 16 MI.

24

Delaney

Dog Lake

9600

2

Lembert Dome
9450

9200

TIOGA

BM
9038

BM 9151

BM 9

Tuolumne Meadows
High Sierra Camp
Rapids

Dana

8800

Ranger Station

BM
8592

N E

M E A D O W S

Campground

Footbridge

8800

N A L

Lyell

Unicorn Cr.

see MAP 23

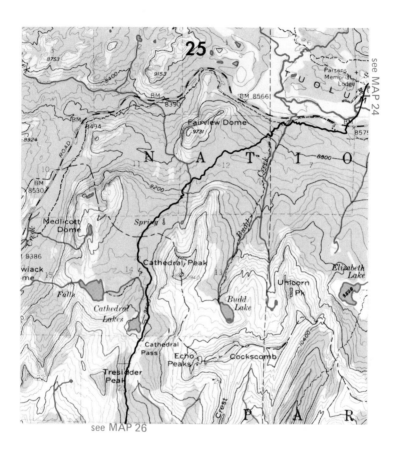

see MAP 24

see MAP 26

8753

8400

9153

Parsons
Memorial
Lodge

T U O L U

BM
8390

BM 8566

BM
8494

Fairview Dome
9731

BM
8924

BM
8575

ROAD

N   A   T

I   O

8800

10

11

12

7

O

BM
8530

9200

Spring

Budd Creek

Medlicott
Dome

Elizabeth
Lake

8386

8 Spring

Cathedral Peak

Budd

14

13

Unicorn
Pk

9520

wiack
me

15

9940

8500

Falls

Cathedral
Lakes

Budd
Lake

Cathedral
Pass

Echo
Peaks

Cockscomb

10400

Tresidder
Peak

Crest

P   A   R

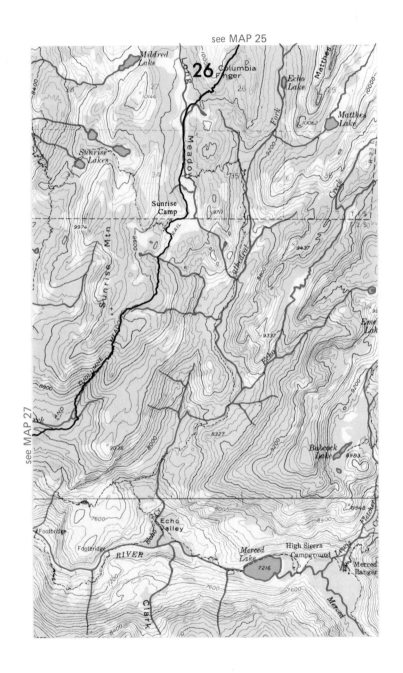

see MAP 27

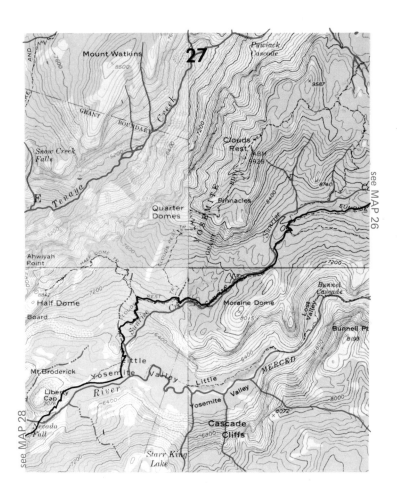

see MAP 26

see MAP 28

Mount Watkins

8500

Pinciack
Cascade

9587

Clouds
Rest

BM
9926

8740

Snow Creek
Falls

5200

6600

E

Tenaya

Pinnacles

8400

SUNRISE

Quarter
Domes

GRANT

BOUNDARY

Creek

YOSEMITE

Ahwiyah
Point

7200

HALF DOME

7200

8844

Half Dome

Board

REST

Sunrise

Moraine Dome

9015

Bunnel
Cascade

Lost Valley

Bunnell Pt
8193

Mt.Broderick

Yosemite

Little

Valley

6400

Little

MERCED

6400

8000

Liberty
Cap
7076

River

6400

Yosemite

Valley

6800

Cascade
Cliffs

9072

Nevada
Fall

7200

Starr King
Lake

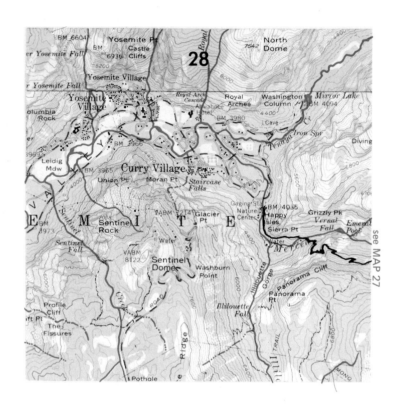

see MAP 27

Cumulative Mileage Table for Official JMT Route and Mt. Whitney Trail
(includes out-and-back to/from Mt. Whitney's summit)

Point Description	N→S	Dist. btwn. pts.	S→N
Happy Isles	0.0		218.3
Little Yosemite Valley	4.4	4.4	213.9
Sunrise High Sierra Camp	13.7	9.3	204.6
JMT-Cathedral Lakes jct.	21.0	6.3	197.3
Rafferty Creek crossing	24.9	3.9	193.4
Lyell Fork base camp	32.1	7.2	186.2
Donohue Pass	37.1	5.0	181.2
Rush Creek Forks/Trail jct.	40.9	3.8	177.4
JMT-PCT jct., Thousand Island Lake	44.2	3.3	174.1
Shadow Creek footbridge	49.7	5.5	168.6
Footbridge near Reds Meadow	57.6	7.9	160.7
Duck Pass jct.	70.1	12.5	148.2
Tully Hole	76.4	6.5	141.9
Silver Pass	81.2	4.8	137.1
Footbridge over Mono Creek	88.2	7.0	130.1
Jct. with trail to Bear Diversion Dam	94.4	6.2	123.9
Selden Pass	101.5	7.1	116.8
Jct. with lateral to Florence Lake Trail	107.4	5.9	110.9
Jct. with Florence Lake Trail	109.1	1.7	109.2
Jct. with Piute Pass Trail	110.9	1.8	107.4
McClure Meadow in Evolution Valley	118.2	7.3	100.1
Evolution Lake inlet	123.1	4.9	95.2
Muir Pass	127.7	4.6	90.6
Jct. with Bishop Pass Trail	134.7	7.0	83.6
Middle Fork Kings River-Palisade Creek	138.0	3.3	80.3
Mather Pass	148.2	10.2	70.1
Crossing, main South Fork Kings River	153.4	5.2	64.9
Pinchot Pass	157.7	4.3	60.6
Woods Creek Crossing	165.4	7.7	52.9
Glen Pass	174.5	9.1	43.8
Jct. w. trs. to Kearsarge Pass, Charlotte Lk.	176.8	2.3	41.5
Jct. with trail down Bubbs Creek	179.0	2.2	39.3
Forester Pass	187.0	8.0	31.3
Wallace Creek	196.4	9.4	21.9
Southern jct. with PCT	199.8	3.4	18.5
Jct. with tr. to/from Mt. Whitney summit	206.2/210.0	6.4	12.1/8.3
Trail Camp	212.3	2.3	6.0
Whitney Portal	218.3	6.0	0.0

The scale of maps in this book is 1:67,760, or 1″ = approximately 1.1 miles.

Kearsarge Lakes and Kearsarge Pinnacles from Kearsarge Pass

Read This

Hiking in the backcountry entails unavoidable risk that every hiker assumes and must be aware of and respect. The fact that a trail is described in this book is not a representation that it will be safe for you. Trails vary greatly in difficulty and in the degree of conditioning and agility one needs to enjoy them safely. On some hikes routes may have changed or conditions may have deteriorated since the descriptions were written. Also, trail conditions can change even from day to day, owing to weather and other factors. A trail that is safe on a dry day or for a highly conditioned, agile, properly equipped hiker may be completely unsafe for someone else or unsafe under adverse weather conditions.

You can minimize your risks on the trail by being knowledgeable, prepared, and alert. There is not space in this book for a general treatise on safety in the mountains, but there are a number of good books and public courses on the subject, and you should take advantage of them to increase your knowledge. Just as important, you should always be aware of your own limitations and of conditions existing when and where you are hiking. If conditions are dangerous, or if you are not prepared to deal with them safely, choose a different hike! It's better to have wasted a drive than to be the subject of a mountain rescue.

These warnings are not intended to scare you off the trails. Millions of people have safe and enjoyable hikes every year. However, one element of the beauty, freedom, and excitement of the wilderness is the presence of risks that do not confront us at home. When you hike you assume those risks. They can be met safely, but only if you exercise your own independent judgment and common sense.

North to South:
Yosemite Valley to Whitney Portal

In the trail descriptions that follow, you will often find a pair of numbers in parentheses — e.g., "(4520 — 0.9)." The first number is the elevation at that point; the second number is the mileage since the last such point.

The "N-S" numbers on each page of north-to-south trail description refer to the map(s) that cover the area being described on that page. (The "S-N" numbers are for the companion south-to-north description.)

You'll probably want to spend a night in Yosemite Valley before you start your trip. Be sure to make arrangements for your room or campsite well in advance! You can't drive to your trailhead, so take the free Valley shuttlebus to the stop nearest the start of the John Muir Trail (JMT): the Happy Isles stop. From this stop, walk south on a paved path, then turn left on another paved path that crosses the Merced River on a bridge. Just on the other side of the river, you'll find a stream-gaging station and a large sign announcing the northern terminus of the JMT and a number of mileages along it. This is your starting point. Get an early start, as the trail can be very hot by midday, and the first legal campsites lie 4.4 miles ahead and 2065 feet up.

From its start (4035 — 0.0) the asphalt-surfaced trail climbs steeply southward and upward on the east wall of the river canyon, passing a couple of junctions with footpaths down to the Happy Isles, two pretty islets in the Merced. You'll have lots of company from here to the junction with the trail to Half Dome! The route curves around Sierra Point and continues climbing, now eastward on the canyon's north wall, high above the turbulent river. You descend briefly to cross the river on a

See Map 28

13

stout footbridge (4520 — 0.9) offering a superb view of Vernal Fall that millions have photographed, and you should, too.

Across the bridge are a drinking fountain — last potable water on the JMT before Whitney Portal! — and restrooms. At a junction just beyond the bridge, the JMT turns south to begin switchbacking steeply up the canyon's south wall, while the Mist Trail continues ahead, along the steep river channel; the trails will rejoin just above Nevada Fall. The scenic Mist Trail is somewhat shorter, significantly steeper, and, in early and mid-season, so wet from spray from Vernal and Nevada falls that hikers must don rain gear or get soaked to the skin — not recommended for backpackers! Taking the JMT, you shortly pass a signed HORSE TRAIL coming in from the west and continue upward under California black oaks, Douglas firs, and bigleaf maples. Pause at Clark Point (5481 — 1.1) to take in the spectacular view; a lateral trail, the Clark Trail, descends from here on rocky switchbacks to meet the Mist Trail a little upstream of Vernal Fall. Continue upward on the JMT, enjoying ever-better views of Liberty Cap, Mt. Broderick, and Nevada Fall as you traverse walled-in sections of trail that cling to the steep, sometimes damp, canyon wall. You can hear Nevada Fall roaring ahead as you pass a junction with the Panorama Trail (5950 — 1.0) as well as junctions with use trails in this popular area, soon emerging on granite slabs just upstream of this fall, which at 594 feet is the Merced's greatest leap. A sturdy footbridge leads over the raging waters, and you follow a line of rocks up the slabs before descending a zigzag to meet the upper end of the Mist Trail near some restrooms.

Head east on the JMT into Little Yosemite Valley on a broad, sandy track, soon reaching a junction where the JMT continues ahead on the right fork and the left fork is a short-cut; you'll meet this shortcut trail again when it intersects the JMT again a little north of the camping area in Little Yosemite Valley. The JMT, under dense forest, roughly parallels the now-unseen river but is separated from it by a crude log fence. Soon the JMT turns north at a junction (6100 — 1.4) in Little Yosemite Valley to pass restrooms and numerous campsites — the first legal sites on the trail; the trail that goes ahead is bound for Merced Lake. A summer ranger is usually stationed here, and the area is a favorite with bears, so there are bear boxes. You shortly intersect the shortcut trail again — its north-

See Maps 28, 27

Vernal and Nevada falls from Glacier Point

east extension from here goes 100 yards to some improved camp-sites on Sunrise Creek — and begin steeply ascending the canyon's north wall.

The JMT meets the lateral to Half Dome (7015 — 1.5) — an incredible four-mile round trip that shouldn't be missed — and in another half mile meets the trail to Clouds Rest (7210 — 0.5) just beyond which are campsites along Sunrise Creek plus an improved site on the low ridge to the east. You shortly ford a tributary which boasts a couple of campsites; use trails to/from campsites in this area are so well-trod they may briefly be mistaken for the JMT. Climbing along Sunrise Creek, camp-sites are surprisingly few. You ford the creek in red-fir forest and, in another mile, reach the junction (8000 — 2.3) with the Forsyth Trail; there are poor campsites on a rise overlooking Sunrise Creek about 200 yards up the Forsyth Trail from this junction.

See Map 27

Continuing up the creek, you cross a giant moraine, the largest of a series of ridgelike glacial deposits in this area, left by the glacier that once filled Little Yosemite Valley. Leaving Sunrise Creek behind, you top a broad, southeast-trending ridge at the south end of Sunrise Mountain before descending the mountain's east slopes to the south arm of beautiful Long Meadow, whose streams may be dry by late season. The JMT shortly curves east to meet a trail to Sunrise Lakes and Clouds Rest, and just beyond this junction passes below Sunrise High Sierra Camp (9300 — 5.0). By taking the trail toward Sunrise Lakes, you'll find use trails leading not only to the camp but to backpacker campsites offering spectacular views eastward of rugged peaks and, of course, of glorious sunrises, over Long Meadow. The JMT curves north up l-o-n-g Long Meadow, climbing gently toward Cathedral Pass, to pass a junction with a trail down Echo Creek (9320 — 0.8).

Traversing the east slopes of Tressider Peak, you find a magnificent view over much of southern Yosemite at the high point of this leg (9940'); the panorama includes the peaks around

See Maps 27, 26

The overhang on Half Dome

Jason Winnett

Vogelsang High Sierra Camp in the southeast, the whole Clark Range in the south, and the peaks on the Park border in both directions far away. You pass under steep-walled Columbia Finger before descending to the broad saddle called Cathedral Pass (9700 — 2.7), from which a trailless swale sweeps away to the south, providing a seasonal flower display that's worth the dayhike from upcoming Highway 120. But first, you descend into the shallow bowl cradling upper Cathedral Lake, set like a jewel among Cathedral, Tressider, and Echo peaks. Camping regulations vary in this area; sometimes upper Cathedral Lake is open to camping and lower Cathedral Lake closed, sometimes it's just the opposite. If upper Cathedral Lake is open to camping, a few pleasant sites may be found high on the forested sides of the bowl cupping it.

You leave upper Cathedral Lake for a gentle descent through moderate forest to a junction with the lateral to lower Cathedral Lake (9460 — 1.1), which may or may not be open to camping — see the observations on camping at these lakes, above. The JMT makes a sandy descent northward, gently traversing the west slopes of Cathedral Peak at first, then dropping more steeply past a robust spring and fording the small stream resulting from the spring. Views through the moderate forest of lodgepole and mountain hemlock include several of the great granite domes — huge *roches moutonées* — for which the Tuolumne Meadows area is renowned. Just before you'd reach Highway 120, you reach a junction (8570 — 2.7) with a trail that leads east to roughly parallel the highway but which keeps well south of it. Turn east on this trail, almost immediately cross Budd Creek on a footbridge, and stroll through forest to reach another junction (8620 — 0.9). This is a point of some disagreement: all current sources and maps say the route that continues ahead (east) here and stays south of the highway is the official route of the JMT, but, traditionally, the JMT has turned north here to cross the highway and arc through famous Tuolumne Meadows. On one point there is no disagreement: travelers along the highway through Tuolumne Meadows will find a visitor center, a small store, a minimal café, Tuolumne Meadows Campground (the only legal camping in this area, with a few walk-in sites), and Tuolumne Meadows Lodge (showers; reserve meals and lodging well in advance). We'll describe both routes:

See Map 25

Official, current JMT route. Less scenic than the traditional route, but avoids busy Highway 120 altogether. Continue east from the "point of some disagreement" to begin an easy, rolling stroll through moderate forest with a good wildflower display in season. After fording a small stream, you cross bigger Unicorn Creek on a footbridge, pass a use trail to nearby Tuolumne Meadows Campground, and then intersect the trail from the campground to Elizabeth Lake. Use trails radiate to/ from the popular campground in this area. You meet another trail from the campground and soon begin to glimpse Lyell Fork Tuolumne River through the trees. It's not long before you reach a junction (8650 — 2.3) where one fork comes in from the north, from a pair of bridges over Lyell Fork, and the other fork goes ahead, roughly paralleling the river. This is the point where the official, current JMT route rejoins the traditional JMT route.

Traditional JMT route. Much more scenic than the official, current route, but requires crossing busy Highway 120 twice. Turn north toward the highway at the "point of some disagreement," carefully crossing the road and following a well-worn path out into the flowery meadow. You ford a couple of streamlets before crossing the Tuolumne River on a footbridge below a low rise on which you spy some buildings, Parsons Lodge and McCauley Cabin, which you may want to take a look at. The area may be confusing because it's laced with old roads, official trails, and use trails; your goal is to curve east and then southeast through the meadow and back to the highway. Beyond the footbridge you reach a disused road and turn northeast, then east on it, toward the huge granite face of Lembert Dome. At a fork (8590 — 0.5), you go northeast (right), and shortly before the dome, you circumvent a gate that bars vehicle traffic and pass a spur road to the local stables. Keeping to the road, you pass below the dome and through its parking lot to reach the highway (8595 — 0.7). Crossing the highway again, you pick up a wide dirt track that presently becomes a closed dirt road before passing near a large parking lot where, in season, there's a booth from which a summer ranger dispenses wilderness permits. Your path parallels a paved road that passes the Tuolumne Meadows Ranger Station and then passes a spur trail to a large parking lot for backpackers and to Tuolumne Meadows Lodge (8650 — 0.8). Soon you find your route paralleling Dana Fork Tuolumne River and passing one

See Maps 25, 24

and then another spur trail (8690 — 0.3) northeast to the lodge. You cross Dana Fork on a footbridge and quickly reach a junction with a northeast trail to Gaylor Lakes. Staying on the JMT, you curve south and leave Dana Fork behind. The trail presently exits forest as it reaches Lyell Fork of the Tuolumne River, which you cross at a spectacular spot on a pair of bridges, where the views demand a photography stop. In a few more steps you re-enter forest and reach a junction (8650 — 0.6) where the traditional JMT route rejoins the official, current JMT route.

However you got to this junction, you now follow the JMT as it lazily parallels the Lyell Fork eastward, gradually leaving Tuolumne Meadows behind and heading into beautiful Lyell Canyon, where camping is prohibited within 4 miles of the highway. Your next junction (8710 — 0.7) is with the Rafferty Creek Trail, part of Yosemite's popular High Sierra Loop Trail — not to be confused with the High Sierra Trail of Sequoia National Park, whose route you will eventually share as you near the southern end of your journey. Shortly beyond this junction you cross Rafferty Creek on a footbridge. In another 3/4 mile the trail and the river curve south-southeast, and the forest thins till the trail is skirting and sometimes even in the meadows lining the river. You enjoy a wonderfully scenic stroll up-can-

See Map 24

The Unicorn over Tuolumne Meadows

yon and eventually begin to spot campsites here and there. Lyell Canyon is infamous for its marauding bears, and cables that once supplemented trees for hanging your food are being removed because ineffective. All methods of protecting your food are regarded as worthless here except for bear-resistant food canisters.

Just north of imposing Potter Point you reach a major camping area at the junction (8901 — 4.4) with the trail to Ireland and Evelyn lakes and Vogelsang High Sierra Camp. The JMT shortly fords Ireland Creek and continues upstream past more campsites to what's called Lyell Fork base camp (9040 — 2.8), a forested bench just before you begin the steep climb up the head of Lyell Canyon to Donohue Pass. This site is popular with weekend backpackers because of its proximity to the highway.

From Lyell Fork base camp you begin a series of steep, exposed switchbacks that end abruptly at a forested bench with many overused campsites. The trail crosses Lyell Fork (9650 — 1.4) on

See Maps 24, 23

Looking south from Donohue Pass to Banner Peak and Mt. Ritter

a footbridge before resuming its ascent, this time to a charming subalpine meadow blessed with a lakelet. One or two campsites are nestled in the whitebark pines on the sandy rise east of the outlet (10,180 — 1.8), which you ford just below the lakelet. Now you climb steeply away from the west side of the lakelet, leveling out in a marshy region beyond which the JMT pops over a low ridge and then descends to a lovely tarn whose outlet you cross. When still, the tarn picturesquely reflects Mt. Lyell, at 13,144 feet Yosemite's highest, and its glacier, the largest seen from the JMT — though after years of drought and rising temperatures, it may be just a huge snowfield before too long.

Now the JMT tackles the last steep climb eastward to Donohue Pass, along which one or two Spartan campsites may be spotted, usable when seasonal streams provide water nearby. Nearing the top, your route is partly in a long, straight fracture. Rest stops permit enjoying the expansive views until you reach tarn-blessed Donohue Pass (11,056 — 1.8). The pass itself has few views, but as you cross to the pass's east side, leaving Yosemite National Park for Ansel Adams Wilderness, the large granite basin at the headwaters of Rush Creek opens before you invitingly. This part of the JMT is unique: the stretch from Donohue Pass to Island Pass is the only leg of the JMT proper that is east of the Sierra Crest; Rush Creek drains into a Great Basin lake, famous Mono Lake. Down you go, eastward and then southward into the basin, whose meadowed floor is too wet and fragile for camping except for a few Spartan sites on the drier hummocks that dot the basin here and there — sites well worth seeking out. Rush Creek's headwaters, often paralleled and a couple of times forded by the JMT, pour down a series of enchanting, increasingly forested benches where campsites on the higher, drier rises are worth looking for.

A more serious ford of Rush Creek, difficult in early season, precedes the junction with the Marie Lakes Trail (10,030 — 3.0); for those who can safely make the leap with a full pack, there is a jump-across spot just downstream of the ford. There are a couple of fair campsites near this junction. Soon the JMT switchbacks down and southeastward to a junction with the Rush Creek Trail at an area known as Rush Creek Forks. Good campsites are located on the west side of the trail along a bench about 0.3 mile north of the Forks; the sites aren't obvious but are well worth seeking out, considering that camping right at the Forks is very

See Maps 23, 22, 21

poor as well as illegal (too close to water). A summer ranger may be stationed about 5 miles away, below Waugh Lake. From the junction with the Rush Creek Trail (9600 — 0.8) you continue south, making at least three fords in the next quarter mile, some of which can be difficult in early season. Climbing again, through dry forest, you pass a junction with the trail southwest to Davis Lakes before reaching the meadows and ponds of broad, marshy Island Pass (10,203 — 1.5), which commands sweeping views of the dark Ritter Range. Just south of the high point — it's hard to tell which is Island Pass's high point! — the trail winds between a pair of small lakes offering good camping and outstanding views of Banner Peak.

From Island Pass you descend moderately toward big, blue Thousand Island Lake, whose surface is dotted with dozens of rocky islets. As the descent levels out, you reach a junction with a trail that leads around the lake's northwest shore, where there is fair-to-good, though bear-infested, camping. Note that camping is prohibited within 1/4 mile of the lake's outlet. Views of Banner Peak over Thousand Island Lake are irresistibly photogenic and were memorialized in many of Ansel Adams' most famous photographs — how appropriate that this area is now part of his namesake wilderness. A few more steps bring you to a junction (9834 — 1.8) where the John Muir Trail and the Pacific Crest Trail (PCT), which have been one and the same since Tuolumne Meadows, diverge for several miles. The PCT turns east to traverse the western slopes of San Joaquin Ridge, while the JMT continues southeast on a footbridge over the outlet of Thousand Island Lake before beginning a moderate climb past pretty Emerald Lake, whose western shore is closed to camping, and then to Ruby Lake, where there is fair camping.

The JMT climbs again, to the ridgetop above Ruby Lake, before descending on rocky switchbacks to beautiful, windy Garnet Lake, a smaller version of Thousand Island Lake and likewise dotted with islets. Note that, as for Thousand Island Lake, camping is prohibited within 1/4 mile of Garnet Lake's outlet. Fortunately, near the bottom of the switchbacks you find a junction with a use trail that leads to campsites on Garnet's northwest shore — the sites get better the farther you go toward Garnet's head. You trace Garnet's north shore briefly, cross its outlet (9680 — 2.0) on a rickety-looking footbridge, and immediately pass an obscure junction with a rough trail that de-

See Map 21

scends northeast into the canyon of the Middle Fork San Joaquin River. Now the JMT traces Garnet's south shore briefly before turning southeast to climb steeply up the ridge south of Garnet. At a saddle atop the ridge, there's a swimming-pool-sized pond that warms up enough by midsummer for pleasant bathing.

The 1,100-foot descent of the ridge dips through a tiny canyon and passes a few sites suitable for camping when water is available nearby. Near the bottom of the descent, you pass a shady flat near a tributary of Shadow Creek, where fair campsites may be found. The area is a mecca for bears — either "canister" your food or kiss it goodbye. The JMT makes a T-junction (9030 — 2.4) with a trail that heads west to Ediza Lake and east to Shadow Lake and Agnew Meadows. The area, from Ediza to Shadow, has been so overused that most of it is now closed to camping, and the latest regulations are posted where trails first enter the area — be sure to study and follow them to help the area recover. As of 1997, camping along the JMT here was severely restricted and Shadow Lake was entirely closed to camping.

See Maps 21, 20

Banner Peak and Mt. Ritter over Garnet Lake

The JMT turns east and descends a rocky track along rushing Shadow Creek before reaching another junction at the head of beautiful Shadow Lake, where one fork continues east to Agnew Meadows while the JMT turns southeast to cross a handsome footbridge (8760 — 1.1) and curve partway around the lake's south shore before tackling a dusty, switchbacking, 656-foot climb up a steep ridge, this one through dense forest with only occasional glimpses of the Ritter Range. At the top of the climb the trail crosses a small saddle before descending to shady Rosalie Lake (9350 — 1.5), where camping is good but overused. You skirt Rosalie's north and east shores before climbing a little and then dipping down to hemlock-shaded Gladys Lake (9580 — 0.6), which also has a number of good campsites. After passing Gladys, the JMT rolls over a little saddle and begins a long, gradual descent of Volcanic Ridge under mountain hemlocks and western white and lodgepole pines, passing the attractive, marshy Trinity Lakes, a series of shallow ponds strung out along the trail. Dry campsites far enough from water are few, but keep your eyes peeled for them. The JMT skirts lower Trinity Lake (9180 — 1.8) before making a final zigzag drop on pumice footing to a T-junction (8150 — 2.0) with a trail that goes northwest to Minaret Lake and southeast toward Devils Postpile. Just across the trail are boggy Johnston Meadow and little Johnston Lake, a pretty spot to cool off the feet. The JMT turns southeast at this junction and continues descending loose pumice to a ford of Minaret Creek, then passes a junction with a trail west toward Beck Lakes, before descending south-southeast to a large X-junction just inside the boundary of Devils Postpile National Monument, where it is reunited with the PCT, which comes in from the north.

From this junction the rejoined trails have been rerouted onto a singularly pointless, boring, viewless traverse of the west wall of the canyon of the Middle Fork San Joaquin River, a traverse that necessitates your making a detour to see the famous columnar-basalt formation for which the Monument is named. Alternatively, you could take the easier, more interesting, more crowded, original route of the JMT right past the Devils Postpile. We'll describe both routes:

To go past the Devils Postpile, take the lower, southeast-trending fork at the X-junction down to the riverbank, where you soon find a bridge (washed out by floods in 1997 but since

See Maps 20, 19

rebuilt at a slightly different location — follow signs if need be). Cross the river to a junction with the trail north to nearby Postpile headquarters and south to the Postpile itself and, eventually, to Reds Meadow at the south end of the Monument. Turn south and shortly find yourself right below the impressive Postpile, where a short, steep loop trail circles the formation. Continue south beyond the Postpile, enjoying an easy walk on pumice trail through moderate to open forest, mostly out of sight of the tumbling river that's west of you. Numerous trails crisscross this popular area, but persist southward toward Reds Meadow. You shortly reach a junction at 7400 feet near the riverbank, just west of which the official route of the JMT/PCT crosses the river on a footbridge. You rejoin the official route by turning southeast onto the JMT at this junction.

The official JMT route takes the upper, south-trending fork at the **X**-junction and begins climbing a very dusty, pumice-strewn track up the canyon wall, nearly viewless because of dense forest. You pass a junction with the southwest-trending King Creek Trail and finally begin dropping on dusty switchbacks past some little meadows to the river, where you cross a footbridge and almost immediately reach a junction (7400 — 2.0) where the official and "Postpile" routes rejoin. (Those wishing to take the official route but still see the Postpile should detour from the **X**-junction as described for the "Postpile" route above, as far as the Postpile, about 3/4 mile, and then retrace their steps to the **X**-junction.)

From this junction at 7400 feet, the JMT leaves Devils Postpile National Monument and heads southeast away from Reds Meadow through a pumice-dusted area of open lodgepole forest that's laced with use trails, mostly radiating to/from nearby Reds Meadow Resort (showers, store, café, lodging — the most accessible resort the JMT passes near) and Reds Meadow Campground, where there are free showers fed by nearby Reds Meadow Hot Springs. The campground, which has walk-in spots for backpackers, is probably your best camping choice in this area. Also, seasonal shuttlebus service (fee) with numerous stops in the Devils Postpile area connects the Monument with Mammoth Mountain Ski Area/Bike Park (see Appendix B). You soon step across a broad trail southbound for classic, 101-foot Rainbow Falls — well worth the 2-mile detour if you have the energy — and for Fish Creek. It's a short dis-

See Map 19

Devils Postpile   _Jeffrey P. Schaffer_

tance north on this same trail to Rainbow Falls Trailhead and a shuttlebus stop.

Staying on the JMT, you begin a loose ascent on a dusty pumice trail on the east wall of the canyon of the Middle Fork San Joaquin River, through an area denuded of its forest cover by the 1992 lightning-caused Rainbow Fire. On the way, you leave Ansel Adams Wilderness and enter John Muir Wilderness. The absence of forest cover has, for now, led to astonishing wildflower displays in season. Roads and use trails crisscross the region, mostly related to the resort, which is about half a mile north of the JMT at this point. Notably, 250 yards beyond the Rainbow Falls Trail, you intersect a road to the resort, then in 100 more yards a use trail to the resort, and in another 200 yards another road that leads 1/2 mile north to the resort. Take your pick!

Camping is impractical along this climbing stretch of the JMT, due to the dense undergrowth; it's also unnecessary due to the proximity of the resort and the campground. Leaving them behind, you ford four branches of Boundary Creek, skirting a dramatic pond that's the source of the southernmost branch. The trail makes a couple of switchbacks, fords a tributary of Crater Creek, and brushes against Crater Creek at a hairpin turn. Near the end of the uppermost switchback leg, the JMT reaches the northern of the Red Cones, a classic volcanic cinder cone with several use trails up its slopes — the ascent is optional but highly recommended — and a junction with a trail northeast to Mammoth Pass.

Those who ascend the northern Red Cone will enjoy sensational views from its top. They include hulking Mammoth Mountain, on whose slopes as many as 18,000 skiers, most of them from Southern California, may be found on a busy winter day, and increasing numbers of mountain bikers on a busy summer day. Mammoth Mountain is a dormant volcano about 220,000 years old, sitting on the west edge of the Long Valley Caldera, which was formed about 760,000 years ago by an eruption so huge that ash from it is found as far east as Nebraska. The area from the caldera north to Mono Lake, including the upper canyon of Middle Fork San Joaquin River, has been volcanically active for the last three million years. Considering Mammoth Mountain's huge snowpack, it's ironic that the area is also the Sierra's "hot spot." The most recent event is the up-

See Map 19

thrusting of Paoha Island in Mono Lake some 250 years ago.

Immediately beyond the junction the trail fords Crater Creek (8700 — 3.6) at the foot of well-flowered Crater Meadow and begins ascending the creek through a little ravine at the foot of the more forested, southern Red Cone, which offers few views. After fording Crater Creek again, you emerge at lovely Upper Crater Meadow and find another junction (8920 — 0.9) with a trail north to Mammoth Pass. A faint track northwest at this junction is about all that is left of a former route of the JMT; taking it leads to campsites on a forested rise on the meadow's north edge, while other campsites are found in the forested fringes around the meadow.

From Upper Crater Meadow the JMT crunches south-southeast over pumice, climbing very gradually before dropping a little to pass a junction with a lateral up Deer Creek and then to ford Deer Creek (9120 — 2.2), which boasts a number of poor-to-fair campsites overused by stock parties. Fill your water bottles at Deer Creek, for the next reliable water is at Duck Creek, nearly six miles away! From Deer Creek you climb gradually on pumice along the north wall of Cascade Valley, enjoying glimpses south to the Silver Divide through the moderate forest of mixed conifers. Views get better as you round a west-trending ridge and make an easy descent into the valley of Duck Creek, where poor-to-fair, overused campsites at 10,000 feet cluster near the ford. A little beyond the ford the JMT begins a switchbacking climb past a junction (10,150 — 5.8) with a trail to Duck Lake and Duck Pass, then climbs a little more before nearly leveling out high (10,460′) on the wall of glaciated Cascade Valley to make a viewful and airy traverse around Peak 11348 (Peak 3464T on the *Bloody Mtn.* topo) followed by a rocky descent past a junction with a use trail leading north to campsites on the west shore of beautiful but overused Purple Lake. Leveling out, you pass a junction with a trail that leads southwest, down into deep Cascade Valley, just before you ford Purple Lake's outlet (9900 — 2.3) — difficult in early season. Camping is prohibited within 300 feet of the outlet.

Now the JMT makes a hot, switchbacking climb of the ridge east of Purple Lake before crossing a wide saddle and descending on rocky-sandy footing to lovely, windy Lake Virginia (10,335 — 2.1), where a few exposed campsites are found. The trail curves around the very soggy north end of the lake to

See Maps 19, 18, 17

Lake Virginia

ford its inlet; in early season you may have to detour north up the inlet to find a decent ford. Beyond the ford, the trail climbs gradually upward from Lake Virginia's northeast shore and curves southeast over a broad, sandy saddle before switchbacking steeply down to the alluring meadow at Tully Hole (9520 — 1.9), where there are a few campsites and a junction with a trail that crosses Fish Creek to climb eastward up the creek to McGee Pass. Staying on impressive Fish Creek's west bank for now, the JMT turns southwest down the creek's canyon, presently crossing it on a steel footbridge and shortly reaching a junction (9130 — 1.1) with the Cascade Valley Trail, which, along with campsites here, may be hard to find because of downed trees.

The JMT turns southeast here and begins ascending toward Silver Pass, generally along the creek draining the north side of that pass; there are a few poor campsites in this dank ravine. Near 9700 feet you cross the creek twice, once at a ford and shortly thereafter, at the foot of a charming little meadow, on a footbridge near a campsite. The trail climbs rather steeply again on the north wall of the ravine before leveling out to ford the outlet of Squaw Lake (10,300') and then angle southwest across the lake's basin, a refreshingly open area after the confines of the ravine; there are one or two exposed campsites here. You climb away from Squaw Lake and level out again at a junction (10,550 — 2.5) with the trail from Goodale Pass. The JMT

See Map 17

turns south-southeast to skirt dramatic Chief Lake and ascend switchbacks to signed SILVER PASS (10,900 — 1.2), where the views are simply breathtaking. In early season there may be a sizable snowbank through which you must climb on Silver Pass's north side. Oddly, the sign for Silver Pass is not at the actual low point on this ridge.

Descending southward from Silver Pass into an alpine basin, you spy a small "pothole" lake with sapphire-blue water and then much-larger Silver Pass Lake. About a quarter-mile north of Silver Pass Lake, the JMT fords a tiny stream and curves eastward away from overused Silver Pass Lake, traversing the sandy rise that separates Silver Pass Lake from its tiny, unnamed neighbor to the east. Both are above timberline, but you soon begin a pleasant descent down increasingly forested benches, stepping over unmapped creeklets and noting many good campsites. You ford Silver Pass Creek (9640 — 2.8) above a large meadow and continue downhill, soon beginning a steep, loose, rocky, exposed descent down the west wall of the canyon of North Fork Mono Creek, next to a series of steep cascades on Silver Pass Creek. The trail re-fords Silver Pass Creek on this descent; this is one of the most dangerous fords on the JMT because of dashing cascades and large, wet boulders; a slip here could be fatal. More switchbacks bring you down to a crossing (8940 — 1.2) of North Fork Mono Creek, another very dangerous ford in early season because of swift, deep, icy water tumbling over a rocky streambed; a fall here could be fatal. Having to make two such wretched fords one right after the other seems very unfair!

Your steep descent continues on poor trail, almost immediately passing a junction with a trail to Mott Lake and presently leveling out briefly at lush Pocket Meadow and its good campsites. Down you go, passing a junction (8270 — 1.4) with the southeast-trending Mono Pass Trail, which leads to the canyon of Mono Creek and then over the southern Mono Pass (the northern Mono Pass is on the eastern boundary of Yosemite National Park). The grade eases as you ford North Fork Mono Creek (can be difficult in early season) one last time, just above its confluence with Mono Creek, and approach the next junction, with a west-trending trail that skirts the north side of huge Lake Edison, a reservoir on Mono Creek that's part of a huge hydroelectric project begun early in the 20th Century. At

See Maps 17, 16

Lake Edison's foot, some 5½ miles away, are Vermilion Campground and Vermilion Valley Resort, a hospitable resupply stop for JMT and PCT travelers (see Appendix B); you can cut 4½ miles off your hike to the campground or resort by hiking 1 mile down this trail, through Quail Meadows, a camping area, to a signed spur trail to the landing for a seasonal ferry service (fee). Southbound hikers, who will next tackle the tough, campsite-less north side of Bear Ridge, should consider timing their visits to Vermilion Valley Resort so that they can spend the night along the JMT and get an early start up Bear Ridge.

The JMT veers briefly east, away from the Lake Edison trail junction, to cross big Mono Creek on a steel footbridge (7750 — 1.6). You soon begin the seemingly interminable, waterless switchbacks incised into Bear Ridge's steep north slope, passing from the cottonwood zone along Mono Creek through realms of white fir, aspen, Jeffrey pine, red fir, silver pine, mountain hemlock, and finally lodgepole at the broad summit. Just south of the crest you pass a trail (9980 — 4.6) that leads west to Lake Edison's dam and the road that links Vermilion Valley Resort with Mono Hot Springs, another resort in this area (see Appendix B). The south side of Bear Ridge is well-watered, and though the descending switchbacks again seem endless, there are plenty of wildflowers to enjoy and opportunities to refill your water bottles and cool your feet. A short way down the descent you pass a small, juniper-dotted bench southwest of the trail, with a few campsites and an unmapped, seasonal stream. As the trail's downward grade eases, it fords a tributary of Bear Creek and reaches a junction (9040 — 1.6) with a trail that leads west to Bear Diversion Dam and an OHV route that in turn leads to the road linking Vermilion Valley Resort and Mono Hot Springs (the latter lies on a short spur road about 1 mile south along the "main" road).

Now in the beautiful canyon of rollicking Bear Creek and paralleling the creek on its east bank, the JMT begins a very gradual rise through mixed forest past numerous campsites. After a time you meet the Lake Italy Trail (9300 — 2.0) coming in from the northeast and soon ford multi-stranded Hilgard Creek. A junction (9350 — 1.2) with a trail that leads up East Fork Bear Creek presently follows. The JMT fords Bear Creek (difficult in early season); beyond here, the grade increases to a moderate climb to the foot of charming Rosemarie Meadow

See Maps 16, 15

(10,010 — 1.4), where the trail fords West Fork Bear Creek — avoid a use trail westward on the creek's north bank. In 200 more yards you meet a trail that departs east for Three Island Lake, on the way to which you'll find Lou Beverly Lake, and in another quarter mile you'll find a trail that climbs southwest to Rose Lake. Both Rose and Lou Beverly lakes provide good, secluded camping. Nearer the JMT, there are campsites in the slabs just above Rosmarie Meadow.

Leaving Rosemarie Meadow, the trail climbs steadily, generally southward, to ford the outlet (10,570 — 1.6) of many-islanded, oddly shaped Marie Lake (exposed campsites) and then skirt the lake's west shore before climbing to Selden Pass (10,900 — 0.9), where the immediate surroundings may be barren but the views are thrilling. You descend steep, rocky switchbacks to little Heart Lake's east shore, ford its outlet, Sallie Keyes Creek, twice, and arrive at the upper Sallie Keyes Lake (10,200′); there are good campsites at these lakes. You ford the short connecting stream, traverse the lower lake's west shore, and then ford Sallie Keyes Creek again before descending a little into a large meadow and passing a tiny cabin — a California snow-survey shelter, no trespassing! A spur trail that once went from this meadow down to the canyon of South Fork San Joaquin River far below seems to have vanished.

The JMT curves southeast, descending gradually past the occasional campsite to ford little Senger Creek (9740 — 3.7) before beginning a long, mostly dry and campsite-less,

See Maps 15, 14

Marie Lake from Selden Pass

switchbacking drop southward into the river canyon far below, at last reaching a junction (8400 — 2.2) with a southwest-trending lateral to the Florence Lake Trail. Down this lateral you'll find Muir Trail Ranch, a possible package drop (see Appendix B), and campsites near the river, as well as more campsites and a hot pool (part of Blayney Hot Springs) and a warmish lakelet across the river — dangerous crossing in early season. The JMT veers southeast from this junction to meet the Florence Lake Trail proper (7890 — 1.7). The Florence Lake Trail goes west, but the JMT curves east on a gradual, dry descent well back from the river, to a junction (8050 — 1.8) with the Piute Pass Trail, which goes north through Humphreys Basin and over Piute Pass to North Lake. You cross turbulent Piute Creek on a steel footbridge, leave John Muir Wilderness and enter Kings Canyon National Park, and find a large Jeffrey-pine-shaded flat with numerous well-used and welcome campsites separated by chaparral thickets.

Leaving Piute Creek behind, the JMT begins a gradual southeast-trending ascent of a sunny canyon down which the green waters of the South Fork San Joaquin River roll and tumble over ledges of dark, metamorphic rock. On the canyon's north side, you pass through Aspen Meadow, then presently recross the river on another footbridge, just northwest of which are some campsites. The trail curves south, and it's not long before you reach a junction where the Goddard Canyon/Hell For Sure Pass Trail continues south down the river, while the JMT turns east, fords a channel and then crosses the river again on a log footbridge (8470 — 3.8). Just over the bridge, the JMT hooks briefly north past some campsites before tackling steep, viewful, east-trending switchbacks up the canyon's east wall into one of the Sierra's most exquisite regions, hanging Evolution Valley.

The trail levels out on the south side of Evolution Creek, whose foaming cascades are a refreshing sight after the hot climb. The JMT presently leads to a creek crossing, but don't cross here. This ford, formerly the "official" JMT crossing, has become needlessly difficult and dangerous, because a hole has formed around a large rock in the channel. Instead, keep going east (upstream) on the creek's south side on an obvious use trail that branches off just before the washed-out former ford. The use trail leads past campsites and out into Evolution

See Maps 14, 13

Evolution Creek below Evolution Meadow

Meadow, soon curving out into the meadow to a ford where the creek is slower, much broader, and sandy-bottomed — though it may still be difficult in early season. Make your way across the north side of the meadow to pick up the JMT again. There are numerous campsites in forested Evolution Valley, and ones fringing its three principal meadows are popular for the views they offer.

Continuing your ascent and fording several tributaries,

See Maps 13, 12

you next reach McClure Meadow (9650 — 3.5); a summer ranger is stationed on the slopes north of the meadow. The trail rises over more tributaries to pass just above Colby Meadow (more campsites). It's not long before you ford the multibranched stream that drains Darwin Canyon, and beyond it you begin a steep climb on switchbacks up the head of Evolution Valley. The forest thins and the views open up as you near the top of this climb and pass an unsigned junction with a use trail into Darwin Canyon.

The reward for this climb is to top a little saddle and descend to the north shore of marvelous Evolution Lake, the lowest large lake in beautiful, alpine Evolution Basin. The land here is nearly as scoured as when the ice left it about 10,000 years ago, and the aspect all around is one of newborn nakedness. To the east is a series of tremendous peaks named for Charles Darwin and other major thinkers about evolution — hence the names "Evolution Creek," "Evolution Valley," "Evolution Lake," and "Evolution Basin." The basin has very few campsites, but some of them will be found in stunted whitebark pines along Evolution Lake's north shore. The JMT traverses high above the lake's east shore before descending to ford its wide inlet (10,850 — 4.9) — a ford recently improved but which may nevertheless be difficult in early season. The trail rises south through a landscape of alpine plants and huge boulders, past numerous alpine ponds, to stunning but campsite-less Sapphire Lake. After briefly tracing Sapphire's shore, the trail begins a moderate-to-steep climb of the rocky slope west of the lake. The grade eases as you skirt an unnamed lake with a larger companion to its east, cross the multibranched outlet (11,400 — 2.4) of Wanda Lake, and finally arrive at huge, wonderfully barren Wanda Lake, named after one of John Muir's daughters and clasped by the rugged peaks of Mt. Goddard, the Goddard Divide, and Mt. Warlow. A few tiny tent-sites huddle too near the lakeshore, among immense glacial erratics providing little shelter from the strong winds that sweep across the lake.

Your trail, sometimes faint, follows Wanda's east shore before climbing gradually past Lake McDermand and up to Muir Pass (11,955 — 2.2), where there is a stone hut intended to provide shelter from storms that even in midsummer may dump snow on this pass. Otherwise, camping in the area is prohibited be-

See Maps 12, 11

North to South

cause of human-waste problems. All around are the fierce peaks of the Black and Goddard divides; behind you, Wanda Lake; below you, Helen Lake, named for the other of Muir's daughters. The solitary peaks and lonely, treeless lake basins are painted in the many hues of the mostly Jurassic-age metamorphic rocks that make up the Goddard Divide.

Muir Hut at Muir Pass

Snow may linger on the east side of Muir Pass throughout the summer in some years, but, assuming you've picked a snow-free summer, you descend rocky-sandy switchbacks toward Helen Lake (11,617 — 1.3), a blue near-circle in a treeless, rusty-brown landscape, fording a growing stream five times. The JMT traces Helen's southeast shore before fording its outlet and continuing the rocky descent down Middle Fork Kings River. You ford an unnamed lake's inlet and then its outlet before descending to the meadowed, multi-branched inlet of yet another unnamed lake, near which you may spot the first, stunted trees since Evolution Lake. Crossing the meadowy inlet is a very damp affair, and skirting the lakeshore leads to another descent, this time into elegant, glacially carved Le Conte Canyon. You soon ford the river again — there's a campsite uphill, across the ford — and drop steeply through patchy forest and across a section blasted out of the canyon's sheer, granite north wall. Obvious campsites are few until the grade eases as you approach Big Pete Meadow and

See Maps 11, 10

then, after a short descent, Little Pete Meadow; the latter is larger than the former, and both offer campsites.

The JMT soon reaches a junction (8710 — 5.7) with the Bishop Pass Trail, which climbs very steeply eastward up Dusy Branch, through Dusy Basin, and over Bishop Pass. A summer ranger is stationed nearby. From this junction, you cross turbulent Dusy Branch on a footbridge almost immediately as you continue down Le Conte Canyon. Overgrowth, rockslides, and changes in the regulations about where you can camp around here have eliminated most legal campsites near the JMT, even at beautiful Grouse Meadow, formerly a favorite camping area. Your best bets for camping in lower Le Conte Canyon are (1) below Grouse Meadow on a flat uphill from the trail and just north of a dashing cascade; (2) a small flat on the river side of the trail and a couple of switchbacks north of the upcoming confluence; and (3) a large flat shaded by Jeffrey pines at the confluence (8020 — 3.3) of Middle Fork Kings River and Palisade Creek.

After skirting the flat at the confluence, your trail curves east and immediately begins the moderate climb up noisy Palisade Creek, in the lower reaches of whose canyon overgrowth and rockslides have eliminated potential campsites. The crumbling supports of a footbridge washed out by floods in the early

See Map 10

Grouse Meadow

1980s mark where a trail takes off across Palisade Creek, south-bound toward Simpson Meadow. The JMT continues east up this beautiful canyon with its patches of forest and open mead-ows, and, as you climb, there are occasional, excellent, over-the-shoulder views back to the peaks around the confluence — as well as the occasional stream ford. Nearing Deer Meadow, you ford the stream draining Palisade Basin high above. You find a couple of shaded campsites at Deer Meadow (8860 — 3.7), which is more lodgepole forest than meadow, but pleasant enough anyway.

Leaving Deer Meadow, you ford multibranched Glacier Creek, exit forest cover, and tackle the steep, rocky switchbacks of the "Golden Staircase," built on the cliffs of the gorge of Pali-sade Creek. This section was the last part of the Muir Trail to be constructed, and it is easy to see why. Views from the ascent are inspiring. The grade eases in a pretty alpine meadow just below lower Palisade Lake, where you have your first awe-in-spiring view of the 14,000-foot Palisades group, knifing sharply into the sky, and of the cirque cradling the lakes. After fording a couple of tributaries, you reach the west end of lower Pali-sade Lake (10,613 — 3.0), where there is poor camping. The trail bends southeastward as it switchbacks up to a viewful traverse high above the northeast shores of both lakes, fording an occasional stream. About midway along upper Palisade Lake you make a ford (may be difficult in early season) of a stream that bisects the bench (10, 880') just above the trail. Several view-rich, exposed campsites along with stunted whitebark pines dot this lovely bench.

Continuing, you pass poor campsites one-fourth mile south-east of the lakes before beginning a very rocky ascent on poor trail to Mather Pass, where snowbanks may linger into late sea-son and winter "washouts" can force some talus-scrambling until they're repaired. At Mather Pass (12,100 — 3.5) — named for Stephen Mather, first head of the National Park Service — the views are breathtaking, if you have any breath left to take. You descend moderately and generally south toward the alpine mead-ows of lake-dotted Upper Basin on switchbacks, curving east near the basin floor before turning south again and beginning a gradual stroll over the tundra, past numerous ponds, and hop-ping over many of the little streams that are the headwaters of South Fork Kings River. Exposed campsites abound in this ba-sin, where there are enough ponds that you can pretty much

See Maps 10, 9, 8

have your own private lakelet. East of the trail, on the Sierra crest, looming Cardinal Mountain (13,397') is named for its reddish tint but is in fact half white and half dark, in a strange mixture of metmorphosed Paleozoic rocks. Forest cover increases as you descend, and you ford the infant river (10,840 — 3.0) near some good campsites. You resume your way downstream, fording the occasional tributary, passing potential campsites, and discovering that a junction with a former lateral to the Taboose Pass Trail and, farther down, a junction with the long-gone South Fork Trail, have both disappeared.

The JMT soon fords the main South Fork Kings River (10,098 — 2.2) — can be very difficult in early season, but look downstream where the river splits around an islet — almost immediately fords a tributary, and begins a steady, switchbacking climb southeast up to the basin holding Lake Marjorie. You meet a junction with the Taboose Pass Trail (10,794 — 1.3) 200 yards before fording a burbling stream. About 20 yards south of the ford you pass the unsigned junction with the trail west to Bench Lake, which is on a true bench high above South Fork Kings River's canyon and which offers good campsites that are off the beaten track. The JMT resumes its southeastward climb from the junction, passing four lakelets and possible campsites, and fording several small streams along the way. A summer ranger is stationed across the outlet of the lowest lakelet. You brush against Lake Marjorie's outlet (11,160

See Maps 8, 7

Just south of Pinchot Pass

— 1.3) at timberline, where you'll find the last couple of campsites before Pinchot Pass, and then follow the lake's east shore
before climbing through alpine meadows to make a final steep,
switchbacking ascent to Pinchot Pass (12,130 — 1.7).

Looking south from Pinchot Pass, you take in a magnificent view: a basin, bounded by glorious peaks on 3½ sides.
The basin's numerous lakes and streams drain south into Woods
Creek and then into the Kings River. Down you go on tight
switchbacks, then across flower-strewn alpine meadows, fording
a streamlet here and there. The JMT curves east to traverse
above an enchanting series of ponds and lakes — come back
just to visit them some day! — before turning south into forest
and descending past more ponds. You pass an unsigned use
trail northeast to Twin Lakes — reputedly a bear heaven —
and shortly reach the unsigned junction with the Sawmill Pass
Trail (10,347 — 3.8); a few exposed campsites lie on the bench
just east of this junction, across the multistranded creek. Descending more steeply now, the JMT drops into the sunstruck,
southwest-trending canyon of Woods Creek, passing a good
campsite near 9850 feet, just where the trail leaves forest cover;
glance east to see the fine waterfalls on the outlet of unseen
Woods Lake. The grade moderates and the trail generally stays
well above the creek. Campsites are few on this stretch, except
for a packer site near 9280 feet. Water is available where you
ford tributaries, and a handsome waterfall on Woods Creek
around 9440 feet is a refreshing sight. The trail presently
plunges very steeply to Woods Creek's north bank below its
confluence with South Fork Woods Creek. Here you find a junction with a trail that goes south down Woods Creek to Cedar
Grove Roadend.

Staying on the JMT, you turn southeast on the overgrown
north bank to cross roaring Woods Creek (8547 — 3.9) on an
imposing, narrow, and very bouncy suspension bridge, "the
Golden Gate of the Sierra," completed in 1988 and not subject
to washouts like its predecessor. One person at a time, please!
On the south bank you find many overused campsites and a
couple of bear boxes under Jeffrey pines. The JMT passes
through this camping area to round the imposing north face of
King Spur, and begins a moderate-to-steep ascent of the lightly
forested canyon of South Fork Woods Creek, staying well away
from Woods Creek itself. You ford the broad stream — may be

See Maps 7, 6

difficult in early season — from Lake 10296 (Lake 3144 on the metric Mt. Clarence King topo) and then several more unnamed streams. In spite of the water, legal campsites are few, and wood fires are prohibited between 10,000 feet and Glen Pass. As the trail approaches Dollar Lake, you pass the unsigned junction with the Baxter Pass Trail (10,230 — 3.7), heading east across Dollar's outlet, and typically find a sign listing the regulations for this scenic but very overused area, considered part of the Rae Lakes basin. Fish haven't been planted in the basin since 1977; the naturalized population is 95% brook and the rest rainbow, typically 8 inches but sometimes as large as 10 inches. For now, camping is restricted mainly to sites near bear boxes; in the future, there may be more latitude for travelers using bear-resistant food canisters. Hanging your food to protect it is utterly useless throughout the Rae Lakes! Camping is severely restricted at Dollar Lake — limited to spots in the boulders above the lake — which has been particularly overused.

Besides, better camping lies ahead, so on you go, soon fording South Fork Woods Creek just below Arrowhead Lake, where there are good campsites and a bear box. The JMT ascends past an unnamed pond to the lowest Rae Lake, where campsites and a bear box are found on the broad, shallow peninsula about midway along the lake. About one-third of the way above the shore of the middle Rae Lake, the trail passes a junction (10,597 — 2.6) with a signed lateral to the Rae Lakes summer ranger station. At this lake, you'll find campsites and bear boxes on the broad peninsula near the lake's south end. Just beyond the use trail to these sites you pass an unsigned lateral to Dragon Lake and then curve west along the north shore of upper Rae Lake, whose shores are too marshy or too rocky for camping. The JMT crosses the "isthmus" between middle and upper Rae Lakes, fording the stream connecting them (difficult in early season) and meets a junction with the unsigned Sixty Lake Basin Trail, where another set of camping regulations is usually posted.

From this junction, the JMT shortly attacks the steep, rocky, switchbacking climb to Glen Pass, fording the outlet of a small lake basin to the west. The higher you rise, the more often you should pause to enjoy the view northward: great peaks dominating a barren, rocky, brown, lake-speckled world with precious little green of tree or meadow visible — and yet, hav-

See Maps 6, 5

ing just passed through it, you know the area is rich with beautiful lakes and streams, with trees, meadows, and wildflowers. The final few switchbacks are very steep and exposed, but you finally stand atop windy, narrow Glen Pass (11,978 — 2.8). The view south isn't nearly as inspiring, but, watching your footing, you wind steeply down past a couple of pothole lakes and a seasonal alpine stream near which there are a very few, very Spartan campsites. You curve west on a moderate grade to traverse high above beautiful Charlotte Lake, enter sparse lodgepole forest, pass a junction with a shortcut southeast to Kearsarge Pass (best route to the pass for southbound hikers), and on a sandy flat meet a junction (10,710 — 2.3) with trails east to Kearsarge Pass and southwest to Charlotte Lake (good camping; bear boxes).

The JMT continues south from this junction, curving a bit east before descending very steeply into dense forest to a junction (10,530 — 0.7) with a trail northeast to Bullfrog Lake (closed to camping) and the Kearsarge Lakes. The JMT continues dropping south into the canyon of Bubbs Creek, twice

See Map 5

Glen Pass

fording Bullfrog Lake's outlet, to Lower Vidette Meadow and a junction (9550 — 1.5) with a trail west down Bubbs Creek to Cedar Grove Roadend. After descending to the canyon floor, the trail curves almost levelly southeast between the Kearsarge Pinnacles and East Vidette, roughly paralleling Bubbs Creek and crossing another Bullfrog Lake outlet, into Vidette Meadow (9600 — 0.7), where there are shady campsites, two bear boxes, and sometimes a summer ranger. Now the grade becomes gradual-to-moderate and the forest cover thins as you ascend beside the wonderful cascades and pools of upper Bubbs Creek to upper Vidette Meadow at 9900 feet, where there are good, well-used campsites and a bear box. More good campsites are located near the several tributaries you ford as well as along the main creek. You reach the unsigned junction (10,500 — 2.8) with the Center Basin Trail going uphill eastward into the eponymous basin. Just beyond, the JMT passes above several overused campsites and a bear box, then fords Center Basin Creek (high in early season). Wood fires are prohibited above 10,800 feet in this drainage. Nearing timberline, you step over a pair of seasonal streamlets and pass a campsite just west of the trail at 10,950 feet, and a little farther on notice campsites clinging a bit like mud-swallows' nests to the canyon wall below the trail at 11,250 feet.

Above timberline now, the JMT strikes east across an alpine meadow, near a shallow, gravelly stream — the infant Bubbs Creek. After a couple of climbing switchbacks, the trail turns south, fords the stream, and begins a moderate-to-steep climb past a small lake and over the creek again, and then ascends a series of benches thickly strewn with boulders. Campsites in this narrow, stony cirque are rare, very Spartan, and probably best suited for those unafraid of rockfall. You ford the creek one last time just below Lake 12248. Now the trail zigzags up to traverse the loose slope west of Lake 12248, on which snow may linger very late, to windswept Forester Pass (13,120 — 4.5), on the Kings-Kern Divide and the border between Kings Canyon and Sequoia national parks. Wearing your wind garments, you enjoy the well-earned, sweeping views from this pass. Technically, Forester is the highest pass on the JMT, and it's certainly the highest pass on the PCT, but your journey will carry you over a still-higher pass before you descend Mt. Whitney's east face.

See Maps 5, 4

Stepping into Sequoia National Park, you descend numerous exposed switchbacks, some of which are literally cut into the rock, down to the foot of a great granite headwall where the trail's grade eases as it passes barren basins full of high, rockbound lakes, where rare, very Spartan campsites may be found. Entering a patch of forest, you step across a stream and spot a fair campsite, then reach a junction with the Lake South America Trail (11,160 — 4.3). It's not long before you descend to the west bank of Tyndall Creek to find a camping area with a bear box; campfires are prohibited within 1200 feet of the crossing. The ford of Tyndall Creek is formidable, and just beyond it you meet a junction with a trail south down Tyndall Creek, where there is a summer ranger station manned in some years. In a few steps there's a junction with the Shepherd Pass Trail (10,840 — 0.7) northbound over the eponymous pass. Shortly, the trail zigzags up to ford the outlet of Tyndall Frog Ponds, visible to the north, where there are fair campsites, warmish swimming, and a bear box — campfires are prohibited within 1200 feet of the ponds.

Now the JMT makes an up-and-down, sandy traverse on the high bench east of Kern Canyon, passing striking Tawny Point before ascending the wide saddle northeast of Bighorn Plateau. Views from here are indeed panoramic! An unnamed, grass-fringed lake atop the gravelly, lupine-streaked plateau makes for great morning photographs westward over it. Next you descend the ground moraines left by the Wright Creek glacier to a sandy meadow on a tributary of Wright Creek. After

See Maps 4, 3

Forester Pass from the south

fording the tributary, the trail climbs over a low ridge and then descends to the main Wright Creek (10,790 — 3.7) and a good campsite. The ford of Wright Creek is difficult in early season.

Another climb follows, and you cross a forested flat before descending into the drainage of Wallace Creek to find a junction (10,390 — 0.7) with the High Sierra Trail, which goes west to Giant Forest from here as well as joining the JMT southward and eastward to the summit of Mt. Whitney. An unsigned use trail here heads east up Wallace Creek to Wallace Lake. The JMT fords Wallace Creek, difficult in early season, to reach popular campsites and a bear box on the creek's south bank. Switchbacking southward away from Wallace Creek, the JMT fords several trickles on its way up to the sandy saddle (10,964 — 1.7) west of Mt. Young. Occasional views across unseen Kern Canyon to the Great Western Divide and Kaweah Peaks Ridge reveal the one of the Sierra's grandest landscapes. The trail winds among the huge boulders of a glacial moraine on this west shoulder of Mt. Young and then descends a little to skirt Sandy Meadow, stepping over its seasonal streamlets. Then the JMT climbs over a ridge radiating southwest from Mt. Young and forested with foxtail pines before descending to a junction (10,880 — 1.7) with the trail up Mt. Whitney's west side. Here the JMT and the PCT part company for the last time, as the JMT turns east, along with the High Sierra Trail, and the PCT continues south toward the Mexican border. The JMT and its camping areas here can be very crowded during the summer.

Turning east on the JMT, you ascend a bench dominated by large foxtail pines, staying above Whitney Creek's north bank. Campsites are found near a junction with a lateral (10,660 — 0.8) that descends to ford Whitney Creek, on the far side of which there is a bear box and a second lateral, this one north to Crabtree Ranger Station. The first lateral continues to Crabtree Meadow (campsites; bear box) to meet the PCT south of where the JMT left it.

Staying on the east-trending JMT, you ascend the canyon of Whitney Creek, keeping to the creek's north bank, and arrive at small, reflective Timberline Lake (11,070 — 1.4), where camping is prohibited but photographing Mt. Whitney mirrored in its still waters is to be encouraged. Skirting Timberline Lake's north shore, the JMT rises into an alpine meadow, leaving the trees behind as it climbs toward Guitar Lake. The trail stays

See Maps 3, 2

well above the lake as it cross higher Arctic Lake's outlet (11,483 — 1.3). Look for campsites above the "guitar's neck" as well as up around Arctic Lake's outlet. Now you climb to the bench above Guitar Lake, where there are a couple of poor campsites near a pair of tiny ponds. After crossing an alpine meadow, the trail rises on long, rocky switchbacks that cling to Mt. Whitney's west slopes. Beside the trail, large yellow flowers called hulsea, or Alpine gold, have anchored themselves in the most unlikely places. Expansive views westward make for pleasant rest stops.

Gasping in the thin air, you arrive at last at the junction (13,560 — 2.9) with the trail to Mt. Whitney's summit. Many backpackers shed their packs here in favor of daypacks with just the necessities — including water, food, and warm clothing — for the 3.8-mile round trip to the summit. With or without your full pack, you turn north on this rugged, final leg of the JMT and in about 20 yards pass a use trail that descends very steeply to high, dry campsites clinging to the rocky west side of Mt. Whitney. You wind among large blocks of talus, pass-

See Map 2

The west face of Mt. Whitney over Timberline Lake

ing Class 3-4 Mt. Muir — "The Sierra's most insignificant 14,000-footer," huffs one writer who feels John Muir has thus been slighted. Hikers enjoy astonishing views westward, where the striking Hitchcock Lakes huddle under the steep, fluted slopes of Mt. Hitchcock, as well as eastward through the notch-like windows around Day and Keeler needles, down to barren glacial cirques containing brilliant turquoise lakes, over Consultation Lake and beyond it to the Owens Valley and the town of Lone Pine, 10,000 feet below. Multiple routes confuse your final climb to the broad plateau that is Whitney's summit, but the sight of the metal-roofed summit building guides you to the top (14,491 — 1.9). Sign the summit register just outside the building, but stay out of the building in a thunderstorm: the metal roof conducts lightning to its occupants, and some have been killed here. The true summit is a little east of the building, reached by scrambling among huge, flattish boulders. The summit on a summer's day is very crowded — there's even a pit toilet north of the building! — but nothing can detract from the incredible views from this highest point in the Sierra Nevada, which also happens to be the official southern terminus of the JMT.

But the end of your trip lies some 6,000 feet below, so retrace your steps to the junction and turn east, leaving the official JMT, for 0.1 more mile to the highest pass on this journey, Trail Crest (13,620 — 2.0 from the summit), where you leave Sequoia National Park and enter John Muir Wilderness. From Trail Crest the Mt. Whitney Trail, exposed and rocky, angles east around the top of a steep chute before beginning an interminable series of tight switchbacks down the mountain's east face. A short section about halfway down is notorious for being ice-covered most of the time, and there is a cable you can cling to if necessary. The powder-blue flower heads of a fragrant phlox called "sky pilot" brighten the gray trail, the building of which required much blasting with dynamite — the natural fracture planes of the granite are evident in the blasted slabs. Finally, the grueling 1600-foot descent ends at barren Trail Camp (12,000 — 2.2), the highest of the legal camping areas along the Mt. Whitney Trail. Numerous hard tent-sites huddle among the giant boulders here, and there are a pair of solar toilets at the east end of the camp. Food must be protected from marmots here. Below the camp you descend some poured concrete

See Maps 2, 1

steps, then continue steeply down a granite trail, finding ivesia, cinquefoil, creambush, currant, and gooseberry growing in cracks in the boulders. The outlet of Consultation Lake cascades down the ravine southeast of the trail. You ford Lone Pine Creek to pass a tiny meadow bright with shooting stars — camping prohibited — and switchback down to sparse timber, finally leveling out near Mirror Lake (10,650 — 2.0), cradled in its cirque beneath the south face of Thor Peak and closed to camping. You make a rocky ford of the lake's outlet and descend again, this time on a slope blooming with senecio, fireweed, pennyroyal, currant, Newberry's penstemon, Sierra chinquapin, Indian paintbrush, and creambush.

Where the trail levels out, you ford Lone Pine Creek and enter a large meadow and camping area, Outpost Camp (10,367', called "Bighorn Park" on some maps). Like Trail Camp, Outpost Camp has a pair of solar toilets. The trail curves southeast along Outpost Camp's upper edge, passing several campsites, then turns northeast to trace the meadow's edge and cross the creek twice in quick succession. Leaving Outpost Camp, you climb slightly before descending switchbacks through large boulders to a junction (10,080 — 1.6) with the lateral to Lone Pine Lake, visible below (campsites). You pass the junction and shortly ford Lone Pine Creek again before beginning the final, long series of dusty, sunstruck switchbacks through sagebrush, Sierra chinquapin, mountain mahogany, and other members of the chaparral community. Two fords of North Fork Lone Pine Creek — the first may be difficult in early season — provide cool nooks on the hot descent. Breather stops on this leg provide a "Veed" view down Lone Pine Creek's canyon framing the Alabama Hills — a filming location for many western movies. Having exited John Muir Wilderness, you presently reach the paved road loop at shady Whitney Portal (8361 — 2.4), where your ride should be waiting for you. In season, Whitney Portal offers a campground, a picnic area, a small store, a café, potable water, and plenty of parking.

Congratulations — you've made it!

See Map 1

South to North:
Whitney Portal to Yosemite Valley

In the trail descriptions that follow, you will often find a pair of numbers in parentheses — e.g., "(10,080 — 2.4)." The first number is the elevation at that point; the second number is the mileage since the last such point.

The "S-N" numbers on each page of south-to-north trail description refer to the map(s) that cover the area being described on that page. (The "N-S" numbers are for the companion north-to-south description.)

Literally, the John Muir Trail (JMT) connects the top of Mt. Whitney — the trail's *official* southern terminus — with Happy Isles in Yosemite Valley — the trail's official northern terminus. But of course you can't drive to the top of Mt. Whitney. Therefore this description of the JMT begins at Whitney Portal, the JMT's *practical* southern terminus, a roadend 13 miles west of Lone Pine, California, where there is adequate parking, a campground, and a small store and café.

From just east of the small store (8361 — 0.0) the route follows the old stock trail from the defunct pack station as it steadily climbs through a moderate forest cover of Jeffrey pine and red fir. Soon the forest cover thins, and the slope is covered with chaparral that includes mountain mahogany, Sierra chinquapin, and sagebrush. This steep slope can get very hot in midmorning, and the trip is best begun as early as possible. Breather stops on this trail section provide a "Veed" view down the canyon framing the Alabama Hills — a filming location for many western movies. Two fords of North Fork Lone Pine Creek — the second may be difficult in early season — provide cool nooks on the hot climb, and you enter John Muir Wilderness.

The trail then turns south and levels off somewhat through

See Map 1

49

several willow-covered pockets having a moderate forest cover of lodgepole and foxtail pines. It passes fields of corn lilies, delphinium, tall lupine, and swamp whiteheads as it approaches a ford of Lone Pine Creek — may be the first water late in a dry season. Shortly beyond this ford is a junction (10,080 — 2.4) with a spur trail that leads east to Lone Pine Lake, which you can glimpse through the trees. Soon the trail turns west up a barren wash and reaches the soggy lower end of Outpost Camp (campsites, toilets; called "Bighorn Park" on some topo maps), a willow-covered meadow that was once a little lake.

The trail fords the meadow's little stream twice in quick succession. At the upper end of the meadow the trail veers away from the waterfall that tumbles down into Outpost Camp from the southwest, crosses the creek again, and then makes a series of switchbacks, past blossoming creambush, Indian paintbrush, Sierra chinquapin, Newberry's penstemon, currant, pennyroyal, fireweed, and senecio. The trail presently fords an outlet and arrives at Mirror Lake (10,650 — 1.6), cradled in its cirque beneath the south face of Thor Peak. This cold lake has fair fishing for rainbow and brook trout, but camping is not allowed here.

Leaving Mirror Lake, the trail ascends the south wall of the cirque via switchbacks that rise to timberline. At the top of the ascent, a last foxtail pine and a broken, weathered, convoluted whitebark snag are seen, along with a few last willows. Some very Spartan, small campsites can be found a short distance south of the trail. Soon Mt. Whitney comes into view over Pinnacle Ridge. From here the rocky trail ascends moderately alongside the gigantic boulders on the north side of South Fork Lone Pine Creek. In the cracks in the boulders, hikers will find ivesia, cinquefoil, creambush, currant, and much gooseberry, and looking across the canyon they will see the cascading outlet of large Consultation Lake. Beside the stream crossing are specimens of the moisture-loving shooting star.

After ascending over some poured concrete steps, the hiker arrives at the last campsites before the west side of the Sierra crest, at Trail Camp (12,000 — 2.0). Here beneath Wotan's Throne is also the last reliable water in late season. There are numerous level campsites and two solar-composting toilets, but no wood. Food must be protected from marmots. Then, as the trail begins seemingly endless switchbacks to a pass on the

South to North

See Maps 1, 2

Sierra crest, unimaginatively called Trail Crest, Mt. Whitney is occluded by a sharp spire, and Mt. Russell, farther north and also over 14,000 feet, comes into view. The rocky, barren, talus slope you are panting up is not *entirely* barren, for in season you may see a dozen species of flowering plants, climaxed by the multiflowered, blue "sky pilot." The building of this trail section required much blasting with dynamite, and the natural fracture planes of the granite are evident in the blasted slabs. Finally the grueling 1600-foot ascent from Trail Camp ends at Trail Crest (13,620 — 2.2), and the hiker suddenly has vistas of a great part of Sequoia National Park to the west, including the entire Great Western Divide. Close underneath in the west are the two long Hitchcock Lakes. To the east, far below, are Consultation Lake and several smaller, unnamed lakes lying close under the Whitney Crest. These lakes may not be free of ice the whole summer.

From the pass, our trail descends on a steep gradient along a very steep mountainside to meet the JMT proper (13,560 — 0.1). Many backpackers opt to shed their full packs here and continue to the summit with daypacks. Turning right on the JMT, you begin the last 1.9 slogging miles to the summit of Mt. Whitney. About 20 yards up the trail to the summit, a use trail descends very steeply to high, dry campsites clinging to the rocky west side of Mt. Whitney. The trail to the summit is rough and exposed at times. In about 1/2 mile on the Class-1 JMT to Whitney's summit, you pass within 400 feet of the summit of 14,015-foot, Class 3-4 Mt. Muir — "The Sierra's most insignificant 14,000-footer," huffs one writer who feels John Muir has thus been slighted. As the JMT winds among the large blocks of talus, you often have views, through notch-windows, of Owens Valley, 10,000 feet below in the east. Closer below are the heads of barren glacial cirques, most of them containing brilliant turquoise lakes. Finally, you see ahead on an almost level plateau a small building near the summit, and with a well-earned feeling of accomplishment you take the last few steps to the highest point in the "lower 48" states (14,491 — 1.9), just east of the building.

Retrace your steps to the junction of the JMT and the Mt. Whitney Trail, don your backpack if you left it, and bear right to begin descending the 1500 vertical feet of Mt. Whitney's west slope on long, rocky switchbacks. Beside the trail, large yellow

See Map 2

South to North

flowers called hulsea, or Alpine gold, have anchored themselves in the most unlikely-looking places.

Breathing thicker air, you reach the bottom of the switchbacks and head northwest along the base of the cirque wall, passing a pair of unnamed lakelets (poor campsites) on a gentle-to-moderate descent that clings to the north wall of this cirque. The trail passes above the north shore of overused Guitar Lake (campsites), crossing its inlet from Arctic Lake (11,483 — 2.9). In early season you may see large golden trout swimming upstream from the lake to spawn, their bodies too thick to be covered entirely by the water of this small stream. Across the lake you have excellent views of the avalanche-scarred north face of Mt. Hitchcock. The avalanche chutes end partway down the face; their lower portions were smoothed off by the passage of the most recent glacier, and have not had time to redevelop since then. Soon your trail reaches timberline, and then descends through a little canyon to small, reflective Timberline Lake (11,070 — 1.3 at the outlet; no camping). The bulk of Mt. Whitney mirrored in the lake is quite photogenic.

From Timberline Lake the trail descends the canyon of Whitney Creek, staying well above the creek, to a junction (10,660 — 1.4) with a lateral to the Pacific Crest Trail (PCT). There are many fair-to-good campsites in this area. Go ahead (west) to stay on the JMT. Going left (south) on the lateral, you would descend steeply and shortly cross Whitney Creek to find a bear box, more campsites, and a use trail left (northeast) to Crabtree Ranger Station (summer ranger on duty); this lateral continues descending along Whitney Creek and meets the Pacific Crest Trail (PCT) at Crabtree Meadow.

Staying on the JMT, you continue southwest through a forest dominated by large foxtail pines to another junction (10,880 — 0.8) with the PCT, on which you turn right (north). From here to Tuolumne Meadows, the JMT and the PCT coincide, except for a stretch north of Devils Postpile.

Northbound now, the JMT soon descends to a mapped stream that stops flowing in early summer. Then, leaving the foxtail forest — ghostly on an overcast day — you skirt what the map calls Sandy Meadow and ascend to a high saddle (10,964 — 1.7). Beyond it the trail winds among the huge boulders of a glacial moraine on the west shoulder of Mt. Young and brings you to excellent viewpoints for scanning the main peaks

See Maps 2, 3

of the Kings-Kern Divide and of the Sierra crest from Mt. Barnard (13,990') north to Junction Peak (13,888'). Soon you descend moderately, making several easy fords, and then switchback down to Wallace Creek and a junction (10,390 — 1.7) from where the High Sierra Trail goes west to a roadend near Giant Forest and a lateral trail goes east to Wallace Lake. The Wallace Creek ford, just north of the popular campsites and bear box, is difficult in early season.

Now your sandy trail climbs up to a forested flat, crosses it, and reaches the good campsites slightly west of the ford of Wright Creek (10,790 — 0.7), also difficult in early season. You then trace a bouldery path across the ground moraines left by the Wright Creek glacier and rise in several stages to Bighorn Plateau. Views from here are indeed panoramic. An unnamed, grass-fringed lake atop the gravelly, lupine-streaked plateau makes for great morning photographs westward over it. Now the JMT descends the talus-clad west slope of Tawny Point past many extraordinarily dramatic foxtail pines. At Tyndall Frog Ponds, tiny lakes beside the trail, there are fair campsites, warmish swimming, and a bear box. Campfires are prohibited within 1200 feet of the ponds. At the foot of this rocky slope a trail goes southwest one-half mile to a summer ranger station and then on to the Kern River, and 200 yards past the junction you come to the Shepherd Pass Trail (10,840 — 3.7) going north-

See Map 3
Between Wright Creek and Wallace Creek

east. Not far beyond is a formidable ford of Tyndall Creek, on the other side of which are campsites and a bear box; campfires are prohibited within 1200 feet of the crossing.

From these gathering places your trail makes a short climb to the junction with the Lake South America Trail (11,160 — 0.7), passes a fair campsite, and rises above timberline. As you tackle the ascent to the highest pass on the JMT and PCT, you wind among the barren basins of high, rockbound, but fish-filled lakes to the foot of a great granite wall, then labor up numerous switchbacks, some of which are literally cut into the rock wall, to Forester Pass (13,120 — 4.3), on the border between Sequoia and Kings Canyon national parks. Wearing your wind garments, you will enjoy the well-earned, sweeping views from this pass. Down the switchbacks you go, unless they are buried under snow, and then stroll high above the west shore of Lake 12248. The trail soon doubles back to cross the lake's outlet and then descends past one or two Spartan campsites fit only for those unafraid of rockfall. You ford splashing Bubbs Creek just below that lake, then ford it twice more within a mile. Soon you reach timber and notice campsites clinging to the canyon wall below the trail at 11,250 feet. You soon pass a campsite at 10,950 feet, just west of the trail before a pair of seasonal streamlets.

Now you ford Center Basin Creek (high in early season), pass several overused campsites (bear box) below the trail, and then pass the unsigned junction with the Center Basin Trail (10,500 — 4.5). You stay on the JMT and ford more tributaries of Bubbs Creek. Many good campsites are located near some of these fords and along the main creek. Wood is scarce, and wood fires are _not permitted_ above 10,800 feet!

Continuing down the east side of dashing Bubbs Creek, you pass Upper Vidette Meadow (9900′), where there are a bear box and good if well-used campsites. At Vidette Meadow (9600 — 2.8), long a favorite camping spot in these headwaters of South Fork Kings River, you find two bear boxes. High use has made the place less attractive, but its intrinsic beauty has not been lost, and the mighty Kearsarge Pinnacles to the northeast have lost only a few inches of height at most since Sierra Club founders like Joseph Le Conte camped here about a hundred years ago. Camping is limited to one night in one place from here to Woods Creek. A summer ranger is sometimes sta-

See Maps 3, 4, 5

tioned in Vidette Meadow east of the trail to assist traffic flow.

Beyond the meadow, a trail goes west to Cedar Grove and the JMT turns north (9550 — 0.7) to fiercely attack the wall of Bubbs Creek canyon. You pause for breath at the junction with the trail to Bullfrog and Kearsarge Lakes (10,530 — 1.5), an alternate and scenic route to Kearsarge Pass for northbound hikers, and then finish off the tough climb at a broad, sandy saddle that contains the junction of the Charlotte Lake and Kearsarge Pass trails (10,710 — 0.7). Charlotte Lake offers good camping, bear boxes, and a summer ranger station on its north shore. In one-fourth mile you pass a shortcut (for southbound hikers) to the Kearsarge Pass Trail, and then you traverse high above emerald Charlotte Lake. As the route veers eastward, it climbs past a seasonal stream, near which are some very Spartan campsites, and then past a couple of pothole lakes, and ascends gently to the foot of the wall that is notched by Glen Pass. It is hard to see where a trail could go up that precipitous blank wall, but one does, and after very steep switchbacks you are suddenly at Glen Pass (11,978 — 2.3). The view north presents a barren, rocky, brown world with precious little green of tree or meadow visible. Yet you know by now that not far down the trail ahead there will be plenty of willows, sedges, wildflowers and, eventually, groves of whitebark, lodgepole, and foxtail pines. To be sure you get there, take special care on your descent from Glen Pass as you switchback down to a small lake basin, ford the lakes' outlet, and switchback down again.

When you are about 400 vertical feet above Rae Lakes, you will see why Dragon Peak (12,995') in the southeast has that name. Where the unsigned Sixty Lake Basin Trail turns off to the west (10,550 — 2.0), the Rae Lakes summer ranger posts the current camping regulations in the Rae Lakes Basin; please study them. The middle and lower Rae Lakes have bear boxes. Hanging your food is utterly useless for protection against bears in the Rae Lakes Basin! Either use the bear boxes or carry and use canisters. (It's hoped that increasing use of bear-resistant canisters will permit campers to disperse more widely, away from the heavily-used bear-box sites.)

The JMT turns east, crosses the "isthmus" between the upper and middle Rae Lakes, fording the connecting stream enroute (difficult in early season), passes the unsigned Dragon Lake Trail, and winds above the east shore of the middle lake,

South to North

See Map 5

passing a signed trail (10,597 — 2.8) to the summer ranger station. Wood fires are not allowed between Glen Pass and 10,000 feet, well below Dollar Lake. Beyond Rae Lakes, your gently descending trail passes above an unnamed lake and drops to the northeast corner of aptly named Arrowhead Lake, where there are good campsites and a bear box. Then it fords gurgling South Fork Woods Creek and reaches scenic Dollar Lake, where there is no bear box and camping is severely restricted to protect its fragile environment. Just north of Dollar Lake, the unsigned Baxter Pass Trail heads northeast across the lake's outlet (10,230 — 2.6).

From the Baxter Pass Trail you descend gently down open, lightly forested slopes, crossing several good-sized though unnamed streams, including the broad creek from Lake 10296 (Lake 3144 on the metric _Mt. Clarence King_ topo — may be difficult in early season). Good, legal campsites are almost nonexistent on this descent. At Woods Creek (8547 — 3.7), on whose south bank there are bear boxes and overused campsites, you cross the torrent on an imposing, narrow, and very bouncy suspension bridge, "the Golden Gate of the Sierra," completed in 1988 and not subject to washouts like its predecessor. One person at a time, please! On the overgrown north bank, you meet a trail to Cedar Grove going south down the creek.

Your reward for all this descent is a chance to start climbing again. As you perspire north up Woods Creek, the steep, exposed trail mostly stays well above the creek — water is available where you ford tributaries — and campsites are few except for a packer site near 9280 feet and a good site where you abruptly enter forest near 9850 feet. After the hard-to-spot, unsigned junction with the Sawmill Pass Trail (10,347 — 3.9), where fair campsites may be found east across the creek's channels, the grade abates. You soon pass a use trail northeast to Twin Lakes, the lowest lakes in the alpine vale where this branch of the Kings River has its headwaters, bounded by glorious peaks on 3½ sides. With one last, long spurt you finally top Pinchot Pass (12,130 — 3.8), one of those "passes" that are regrettably not at the low point of the divide.

From this pass the Muir Trail swoops down into the lake-laden valley below, runs along the east shore of at-timberline Lake Marjorie, where there are a couple of Spartan campsites near its outlet, touches that outlet (11,160 — 1.7), and then

See Maps 5, 6, 7

South to North

passes four lakelets, fording several small streams along the way. A summer ranger station is located across the stream below the lowest lakelet, just south of the unsigned junction with the Bench Lake Trail, which veers west 20 yards before the next ford. Bench Lake, on a true bench high above South Fork Kings River's canyon, has good campsites that are off the beaten track. Just beyond this junction you ford the outlet of all these lakes, and in 200 yards meet the Taboose Pass Trail (10,794 — 1.3) at a sometimes-signed junction on the upper edge of a lodgepole forest. Another downhill segment of forested switchbacks brings you to a ford of South Fork Kings River (10,098 — 1.3), which can be very difficult in early season — but look downstream, where the river splits around an islet.

On the other side, the JMT begins climbing steadily northward into Upper Basin. You cross several unnamed tributaries that can slow you down at the height of the melt, and then ford the infant South Fork (10,840 — 2.2) near some good campsites. East of the trail, on the Sierra crest, looming Cardinal Mountain (13,397′) is named for red but is in fact half white and half dark, in a strange mixture of metamorphosed Paleozoic rocks. West of this peak you cross grassy flats and hop over numerous branches of the headwaters of South Fork Kings River. You can have your own lake or lakelet in this high basin — though the campsites are austere.

This ascent finally steepens and zigzags up to rockbound Mather Pass (12,100 — 3.0), named for Stephen Mather, first head of the National Park Service. The view ahead is dominated by the 14,000-foot peaks of the Palisades group, knifing sharply into the sky. Your trail now makes a knee-shocking descent on poor trail on which winter "washouts" can force some talus-scrambling until they're repaired. Approaching long, blue upper Palisade Lake, you pass poor campsites one-fourth mile southeast of the lake. The route then contours above the lakes, fording the stream draining a high basin to the east-northeast (may be difficult). Viewful, Spartan campsites dot the bench south of this ford and above the trail (10,880′). Beyond the ford, the JMT drops to the north shore of the lower lake (10,613 — 3.5), with its poor-to-fair campsites. Knees rested, you descend again, down the "Golden Staircase," built on the cliffs of the gorge of Palisade Creek. This section was the last part of the JMT to be constructed, and it is easy to see why. In three-fourths

See Maps 7, 8

mile from the bottom of the "staircase" you cross multibranched Glacier Creek and immediately arrive at Deer Meadow (8860 — 3.0), which is more lodgepole forest than meadow, but pleasant enough, anyway.

Beyond the campsites here, the downhill grade continues, less steeply, across the stream draining Palisade Basin and several smaller streams to reach the confluence of Palisade Creek and Middle Fork Kings River (8020 — 3.7), where the crumbling supports of a bridge destroyed by floods in the early 1980s show where a trail takes off downstream for Simpson Meadow. Campsites are few in this lower canyon of Palisade Creek and in the lower part of the next canyon, along Middle Fork Kings River, because of overgrowth and erosion. Look for sites near the confluence, where there is a large, Jeffrey-pine-shaded flat.

The JMT turns north up Le Conte Canyon, staying well above the Middle Fork, and passes more campsites a couple of switchbacks north of the confluence as well as on a flat uphill from the trail and just north of a dashing double cascade. The ascent continues past a series of falls and chutes to Grouse Meadow, a serene expanse of grassland that unfortunately lacks legal campsites. Up the canyon from this meadow, you can see repeated evidence of great avalanches that crashed down the immense canyon walls and wiped out stands of trees. The trail climbs gently to turbulent Dusy Branch, crossed on a steel bridge, and immediately encounters the Bishop Pass Trail (8710 — 3.3) to South Lake. Near this junction is a ranger station manned in summer.

The route up-canyon from this junction ascends between highly polished granite walls past lavish displays of a great variety of wildflowers in season. The trail passes beside sagebrush-clothed Little Pete and Big Pete meadows (campsites at both; the former is bigger) and swings west to assault the Goddard Divide and search out its breach, Muir Pass. Up and up the rocky trail winds, passing the last tree long before you reach desolate Helen Lake (11,617 — 5.7) named, along with Wanda Lake to the west, for John Muir's daughters. This east side of the pass is under snow throughout the summer in some years.

Finally, after five fords of the diminishing stream, you haul up at Muir Pass (11,955 — 1.3), where a stone hut honoring

See Maps 9, 10, 11

Bridge over Dusy Branch near Middle Fork San Joaquin River

Muir would shelter you fairly well in a storm, though the roof leaks. Otherwise, camping is prohibited in the hut's vicinity due to human-waste problems. The views from here of the solitary peaks and lonely lake basins are painted in the many hues of the mostly Jurassic-age metamorphic rocks that make up the Goddard Divide.

From the hut your trail descends gently past Lake McDermand and Wanda Lake, the latter having poor, treeless campsites near its outlet and too near its shore. (Wood fires are banned from Muir Pass to beyond Evolution Lake.) You then ford Evolution Creek (11,400 — 2.2) and descend into the Sapphire Lake Basin, where there are almost no campsites. There is simply not enough ground that is dry, flat, large enough, and stone-free enough to lie down on between Wanda and Evolution lakes! The land here is nearly as scoured as when the ice left it about 10,000 years ago, and the aspect all around is one of newborn nakedness. To the east is a series of tremendous peaks named for Charles Darwin and other major thinkers about evolution, and the next lake and the valley below it also bear the name "Evolution."

The trail fords the inlet (10,850 — 2.4) of long Evolution Lake; the ford has recently been improved but can still be difficult in early season. Stunted whitebark pines at the lake's north

See Maps 11, 12

Mt. Darwin from near Sapphire Lake

end shelter a few, fair campsites. A few hundred yards from them, at a switchback, you pass the beginning of the unsigned trail up to Darwin Canyon and over Lamarck Col, then drop sharply into Evolution Valley. The marvelous meadows in this valley are the reason for a rerouting of the trail through the forest, so the fragile grasslands can recover from over-tromping by the feet of earlier backpackers and horsepackers. After crossing the multibranched stream that drains Darwin Canyon, you pass Colby Meadow, with many good campsites. Farther along, at McClure Meadow (9650 — 4.9) you will find a summer ranger midway along the meadow and more campsites. After further descent and several boulder fords of tributaries, you meet the head of Evolution Meadow and begin looking for a good spot to ford the wide, placid waters (may be difficult in early season). The old ford below Evolution Meadow has washed out. A use trail on the south side leads out of the meadow, past fair campsites, and rejoins the JMT just below the old ford. After passing overlooks of some beautiful falls and cascades on the creek, the trail switchbacks steeply down to the South Fork San

See Maps 12, 13

South to North

Joaquin River's canyon floor and detours upstream to pass campsites and cross a footbridge (8470 — 3.5) over the South Fork San Joaquin River to reach the junction with the Goddard Canyon/Hell for Sure Pass Trail. Staying on the JMT north-west-bound along the west bank of the river, heading downstream, you pass numerous campsites, pass through a stout drift fence, recross the river on another bridge, and stroll past Aspen Meadow. From this hospitable riverside slope, you roll on down and out of Kings Canyon National Park at the steelbridge crossing of Piute Creek — overused campsites on the south side — on the north side of which the Piute Pass Trail (8050 — 3.8) heads north for North Lake.

Between the junction with the Piute Pass Trail and the meadows below the Sallie Keyes Lakes, the JMT is largely waterless and campsite-less for 5.7 miles. However, as the JMT continues west from the Piute Pass Trail junction and away from the river, it reaches a junction with the Florence Lake Trail (7890 — 1.8), and campsites will be found as you head toward Muir Trail Ranch, some 1½ miles northwest on the Florence Lake Trail. Muir Trail Ranch is a possible package drop; see Appendix B. Shortly before the ranch, and about 200 yards west of signs that indicate the JMT is 1½ miles away, both to the east and to the north, an unsigned trail goes south ¼ mile down to riverside campsites. From the campsites on the south side of the river a faint trail goes 150 yards southwest to a natural hot-spring pool — part of Blayney Hot Springs and great for soaking off the grime — and a warmish small lake — great for rinsing off.

From the Florence Lake Trail junction, the JMT veers right to climb the canyon wall. It rises past a lateral trail down to the Florence Lake Trail (8400 — 1.7), crosses little Senger Creek (9740 — 2.2), and levels off temporarily in a large meadow just below Sallie Keyes Lakes. The tiny cabin east of the trail is a California snow-survey shelter — *no trespassing!* A spur trail that once went south from this meadow down to the river valley far below seems to have vanished. Continuing, your route passes the good campsites at Sallie Keyes Lakes (10,200′), crossing the short stream that joins the two. Leaving the forest below, the trail fords Sallie Keyes Creek twice before skirting small Heart Lake and presently reaches barren Selden Pass (10,900 — 3.7). At this pass, many-islanded Marie Lake is the central

See Maps 13, 14, 15

feature of the view northward, and after switchbacking down to skirt its west shore, you ford its clear outlet (10,570 — 0.9), then descend gently to the green expanses of Rosemarie Meadow (10,010 — 1.6), where campsites may be found in the slabs above the meadow. From this grassland a trail forks left, soon climbing southwest to Rose Lake, and about one-fourth mile beyond another trail departs east for Three Island Lake, on the way to which you'll find Lou Beverly Lake. Both Rose and Lou Beverly lakes provide good, secluded camping. About 200 yards past the last junction you ford West Fork Bear Creek (avoid a use trail westward on this ford's north side). After a one-mile descent in lodgepole forest, you ford Bear Creek (difficult in early season).

On the creek's far bank you meet a trail (9350 — 1.4) that goes up East Fork Bear Creek to Seven Gables Lakes, but you turn down-canyon and descend gradually to the multistranded ford of refreshing Hilgard Creek. Immediately beyond, the Lake Italy Trail (9300 — 1.2) climbs east, and the JMT continues down through mixed forest cover, always staying near rollicking Bear Creek. You pass many campsites near the trail, but for more solitude, it is better to find a place to camp across the creek. Below Hilgard Creek (9040 — 2.0), you pass a junction with the trail to Bear Diversion Dam. (Those wishing to go to Mono Hot Springs — see Appendix B — can take this trail west to an OHV route that leads to a paved road; the short spur road to Mono Hot Springs lies about one mile south on the paved road.) The JMT gradually veers west as it follows the contour line, fords a tributary of Bear Creek (difficult in early season), and then turns north at the foot of a tough series of switchbacks

See Map 15

Blayney Hot Springs' hot pool on the south side of the river

up Bear Ridge, where campsites are few. The south-facing hill-side here gets plenty of sun, but it is surprisingly wet even in late season, so that you can pleasure your eyes with flowers in bloom and pleasure your throat with cold draughts — after you treat the water! A juniper-dotted bench not far from the summit offers a few campsites near a seasonal stream. Your route then levels off, and just south of the crest of Bear Ridge passes a trail (9980 — 1.6) that descends to the road linking Mono Hot Springs and Vermilion Valley Resort at Lake Edison (see Appendix B).

The north side of Bear Ridge is incised with seemingly endless switchbacks, which begin in pure lodgepole forest but successively penetrate the realms of mountain hemlock, western white pine, red fir, Jeffrey pine, aspen, white fir, and, finally, cottonwoods at Mono Creek (7750 — 4.6). After you cross the footbridge over Mono Creek, you reach a junction with the trail that goes west to Lake Edison and Vermilion Valley Resort, 1 mile and 5 1/2 miles away, respectively — though seasonal ferry service (fee) at Lake Edison's head, reached by a signed spur trail, can cut 4 1/2 miles off your hike to the resort. Campsites lie several hundred yards west down this trail to the resort.

Beyond the junction, the JMT curves right, soon fords North Fork Mono Creek (difficult in early season), and climbs to a junction with the Mono Pass Trail (8270 — 1.6). Your steep trail levels briefly at lush Pocket Meadow (good campsites), passes a junction with a trail to Mott Lake, and again fords North Fork Mono Creek (8940 — 1.4; very difficult in early season due to swift, deep, icy water and a rocky streambed — one of the JMT's more-dangerous fords, where a fall could be fatal). Then you resume climbing steeply on a narrow, rocky, exposed track up the west wall of Mono Creek's canyon.

The first ford of Silver Pass Creek is very difficult in early season; the combination of slippery boulders and icy cascades make this another of the more-dangerous fords on the present JMT route, and a slip here could be fatal. Above a large meadow you reford the creek (9640 — 1.2) and then rise above timber-line, passing good campsites. The JMT bypasses Silver Pass Lake — contrary to the *Graveyard Peak* topo — staying on east side of the basin as it traverses a sandy rise separating Silver Pass Lake from its small, unnamed neighbor to the east. About

See Map 16

one-quarter mile north of Silver Pass Lake, the trail veers west to ford a tiny, unmapped creek and then continues ascending past the actual pass (low point) to the sign SILVER PASS (10,900 — 2.8) at a glorious viewpoint on the Silver Divide. The descent northward passes Chief Lake and then the Goodale Pass Trail (10,550 — 1.2), switchbacks northeast down to ford the outlet of Squaw Lake (Spartan campsites), passes a small meadow whose outlet it crosses on a footbridge, shortly fords the outlet, and then makes a long, hemlock-lined descent to the beautiful valley of Fish Creek, where there are good campsites near the hard-to-spot junction with the Cascade Valley Trail (9130 — 2.5). Turning right here, you ascend northeast and soon cross Fish Creek on a steel bridge. Staying above this good-sized creek, the route ascends gently to the campsites at Tully Hole (9520 — 1.1), a well-flowered grassland where the McGee Pass Trail departs eastward.

Now the JMT climbs steeply north up a band of Mesozoic metavolcanics which sweep east and grade into the Paleozoic metasediments of dominating Red Slate Mountain (13,163′). Beyond the crest of this ascent, you reach deep-blue Lake Virginia (10,335 — 1.9), with several somewhat-exposed campsites. In early season you will have to wade across the head of the lake or detour rather far north. From this boggy crossing your trail climbs to a saddle below the vertical northeast face of Peak 11147 and then switchbacks down to heavily used Purple Lake (9900 — 2.1), just beyond whose outlet — can be difficult — a trail begins its descent into deep Cascade Valley. Camping is prohibited within 300 feet of the outlet.

From Purple Lake the rocky trail climbs west to an unsigned junction with the use trail leading around the lake's west shore to campsites. The JMT bends north as it levels out high (10,460′) on the wall of glaciated Cascade Valley to make a viewful and airy traverse around Peak 11348 (Peak 3464T on the *Bloody Mtn.* topo). Presently descending, you pass a trail to Duck Lake and Duck Pass (10,150 — 2.2) and then continue to a ford of Duck Creek, where there are undistinguished campsites (10,000′) on both sides of the creek. Fill your water bottles at Duck Creek, as the next reliable water is at Deer Creek, nearly 6 miles ahead.

From the ford of Duck Creek the JMT contours southwest, climbs a little, and then slants northwest on a crunchy

See Maps 16, 17

A very obvious "duck"

footing of loose pumice as it descends through mixed conifers. If you sharpen your gaze, you will see both red firs and Jeffrey pines above 10,000 feet on this north wall of Cascade Valley, well above their normal range. You also have occasional views of the Silver Divide in the south as you slant northwest and

See Maps 17, 18

descend gradually through mixed conifers. Then the trail bends northeast, drops to cross Deer Creek (9120 — 5.8) amid some overused campsites, passes a junction with a spur trail east up Deer Creek, and then leads north through a long meadow overseen by The Thumb (10,286′). Beyond a seasonal stream you meet a trail to Mammoth Pass (8920 — 2.3) in Upper Crater Meadow. At this junction you may see the faint trace of a former route of the JMT/PCT going straight ahead toward a dry rise with some campsites, but the current route veers slightly left to descend a ravine that contains Crater Creek, which you soon ford. After skirting a forested cinder cone, one of the two Red Cones bracketing Crater Meadow, you arrive at expansive Crater Meadow and ford the creek again (8700 — 0.9) to reach a junction with another trail to Mammoth Pass and the other cinder cone, this one less forested and therefore more striking. Use trails lead up this cone, and views from its top are sensational. They include hulking Mammoth Mountain, on whose slopes as many as 18,000 skiers, most of them from Southern California, may be found on a busy winter day, and increasing numbers of mountain bikers on a busy summer day. Mammoth Mountain is a dormant volcano about 220,000 years old, sitting on the west edge of the Long Valley Caldera, which was formed about 760,000 years ago by an eruption so huge that ash from it is found as far east as Nebraska. The area from the caldera north to Mono Lake, including the upper canyon of Middle Fork San Joaquin River, has been volcanically active for the last three million years. Considering Mammoth Mountain's huge snowpack, it's ironic that the area is also the Sierra's "hot spot." The most recent event is the upthrusting of Paoha Island in Mono Lake some 250 years ago.

From the junction by the northern of the Red Cones, your route descends for 2/3 mile to a hairpin turn overlooking an unmapped creek. Several switchbacks later, you curve around a dramatic pond that is the source of the southernmost of four branches of Boundary Creek. Here the gradient lessens considerably, and you ford the branches. Camping is impractical here due to the dense growth, and unnecessary due to the area's proximity to Reds Meadow (below). Charred trees in this area recall the 1992 lightning-caused Rainbow Fire; the near-total destruction of the forest canopy between here and the next major trail junction has made way for an astonishing seasonal flower

See Maps 18, 19

South to North

display. Less than a mile beyond, after stepping over two more rills and leaving designated wilderness behind, you intersect a road on your right that leads half a mile north to Reds Meadow Resort (see Appendix B). Beyond the resort is Reds Meadow Campground, where there are free showers fed from Reds Meadow Hot Springs. Numerous roads, official trails, and use trails crisscross this popular area! Notably, in another 200 yards you pass a use trail branching left, then in another 100 yards another road to the resort, and 250 yards beyond that a trail leading north to the resort and south to Fish Creek. Just beyond is another trail south to Rainbow Falls — a 101-foot sheer waterfall well worth the 2-mile out-and-back detour — and Fish Creek, and north to the Rainbow Falls Trailhead near Reds Meadow Resort. You are now in the general vicinity of Devils Postpile National Monument and, as explained in Appendix B, a seasonal shuttlebus (fee) connects this area to Mammoth Mountain Ski Area/Bike Park. In 1/2 mile from this junction you reach another, from where a trail leads north to Devils Postpile and south to Rainbow Falls. Just beyond, to the west, the JMT/PCT crosses Middle Fork San Joaquin River on a sturdy wooden bridge (7400 — 3.6).

Before you cross the bridge, know that the next official leg is the most pointless and boring of the JMT, featuring poor footing on loose pumice and requiring you to detour to see the area's namesake volcanic feature, Devils Postpile. The JMT formerly went right by the Postpile — it's an easier route, too. We'll describe both routes; there's no significant difference in length:

To go right by the Postpile on the former route, return to the junction just south of the footbridge and turn north toward Devils Postpile. Stroll upriver, passing the famous columnar-basalt formation in a mile. Use trails infest the area, but keep going north. Just beyond the Postpile, you'll intersect a trail leading west to another bridge. Take this trail west over this bridge and then go north to rejoin the JMT in less than 3/4 mile from the Postpile, at a junction described below.

To stay on the JMT, cross the bridge, pass several meadows, and then ascend the west wall of the river canyon on a steep, dusty, pumice path that intersects the southwest-branching King Creek Trail. Dense forest cover obscures most views. You presently descend to the junction where those who went

See Map 19

South to North

directly to the Postpile rejoin the JMT. (A detour south and east from here will get you to the Postpile in just under 3/4 mile.)

From this junction, the JMT and the PCT diverge for several miles. The PCT continues levelly north but the JMT veers left, uphill, and climbs past the Beck Lakes Trail junction to Minaret Creek. You ford this swirling stream and hike one-fourth mile to Johnston Meadow and pretty Johnston Lake (8150 — 2.0). Just past the lake, the Minaret Lake Trail branches northwest, but the JMT turns east, then north, to climb on soft pumice sand up the lake-dotted slopes of Volcanic Ridge, high above the Middle Fork. The first lake you encounter here is lower Trinity Lake (9180 — 2.0), a shallow, pleasant lake set in western white and lodgepole pines. After passing the other, strung-out ponds and lakelets of the Trinity Lakes, the trail goes through a saddle and drops to hemlock-fringed little Gladys Lake (9580 — 1.8), with good campsites. A few minutes beyond you top another saddle and descend to skirt round Rosalie Lake (9350 — 0.6), with more good camps. After a short climb, the trail makes many switchbacks down a cool, north-facing slope that, near the top, offers occasional views through heavy forest of those twin metamorphic monuments, Mt. Ritter (13,157′) and Banner Peak (12,945′). At the bottom of this descent is beautiful Shadow Lake, closed to camping.

See Maps 19, 20

Shadow Lake

After curving around Shadow Lake's south shore, the JMT crosses Shadow Creek on a footbridge (8760 — 1.5) and turns west up the creek's canyon (the east fork goes to Agnew Meadows in the Devils Postpile area; see Appendix B). Camping is severely restricted throughout this area due to years of overuse, and the latest restrictions are posted at points where you enter this sensitive area. In summer 1997, Shadow Lake and the area along Shadow Creek and the JMT were closed to camping.

Soon your route turns north at the Ediza Lake Trail junction (9030 — 1.1) and climbs past fair campsites 1100 feet to timberline, twice fording a small, unnamed creek that may be dry by late season. A swimming-pool-sized pond at the saddle warms up enough in midsummer for pleasant bathing. Then the trail switchbacks down to briefly skirt beautiful Garnet Lake's east shore, passing an obscure junction with a rough trail northeast down to Middle Fork San Joaquin River near the outlet (9680 — 2.4). Camping is not permitted within 1/4 mile of the outlet. You cross the outlet on a rickety-looking footbridge and briefly trace Garnet's north shore before reaching a junction with a use trail that leads to good campsites along Garnet's viewful, windy northwest shore — campsites get better the farther you go.

More switchbacks configure the very rocky trail that climbs north from Garnet Lake to a ridgetop from which you descend to cliff-backed Ruby Lake, with fair camping. Continuing the descent, the JMT passes Emerald Lake, whose west side is closed to camping. Your rollercoaster trail descends once more, this time to dramatic, popular, bear-infested Thousand Island Lake, where camping is not permitted within 1/4 mile of the outlet. A footbridge spans the outlet; just beyond, you find a junction where the JMT and PCT rejoin (9834 — 2.0). You shortly meet a use trail branching around the northwest shore of Thousand Island Lake, where fair-to-good, windy campsites with excellent views of Banner Peak are found, memorialized in some of Ansel Adams' most often seen photographs of this area, now part of his namesake wilderness.

From this junction the route climbs up an easy ridge, utilizing one switchback, and levels off through lodgepole and hemlock trees to reach the meadows and ponds of Island Pass (10,203 — 1.8), immediately before which you find two pretty,

See Maps 20, 21

view-rich lakelets offering good though exposed camping. From here you descend northwest, passing a trail southwest to Davis Lakes, to the junction with the Rush Creek Trail (9600 — 1.5) at the area called Rush Creek Forks. In the quarter-mile trail segment south of the junction there are at least three fords, possibly difficult in early season. In the Forks area, small camps abound, virtually all of them illegal since they are within 100 feet of a creek or trail. A seasonal ranger stationed 5 miles east below Waugh Lake may drop by to enforce the rules. In any event, you will find greater solitude if you avoid the overused camping spots at the Forks. You might also have a little less of a problem with bears, for they tend to investigate the most-used areas first. Good campsites are located on the west side of the trail along a bench about 0.3 mile north of the Forks; the sites aren't obvious but are well worth seeking out.

Leaving the Forks, you quickly engage some short, steep switchbacks that you follow northwest up to a ridge, then cross it and ease up to a junction with the Marie Lakes Trail (10,030 — 0.8), near which you'll find a couple of fair campsites. You ford the lakes' outlet creek just north of this junction; it can be a difficult ford in early season. For those who can safely manage the leap while wearing a full backpack, there is an obvious jump-across spot slightly downstream. After the ford the trail winds up through an increasingly alpine environment, where fair-to-good, though progressively more exposed, campsites may be found here and there on the higher hummocks dotting this series of splendid meadows. The trail curves west and whitebark pines diminish in number and stature as you climb toward a conspicuous saddle — easily mistaken in early season for Donohue Pass. After a wet slog across the tundra-and-stone of our alpine basin, you veer southwest toward a prominent peak and ascend a sometimes obscure trail past blocks and over slabs to the real, signed, tarn-blessed Donohue Pass (11,056 — 3.0).

The Yosemite high country unfolds before you as the JMT descends northwest, partly in a long, straight fracture, passing one or two Spartan campsites usable when a seasonal stream provides a reasonably nearby source of water. You then curve west to a sharp bend southeast, a few yards from which you can get a commanding panorama of Mt. Lyell, at 13,144 feet Yosemite's highest peak, and deep Lyell Canyon. Leaving the bend, the JMT now descends southwest one-half mile to

See Maps 21, 22, 23

the north end of a boulder-dotted tarn that occasionally reflects Lyell and its broad glacier — the largest one to be seen from the JMT. After years of drought and rising temperatures, it may soon be just a huge snowfield. Cross the tarn's outlet, contour along the tarn's west shore, then veer south a little to climb through a gap in a low ridge. You soon begin a steep northward descent of a series of lovely alpine benches that have a few exposed campsites. The descent levels out briefly at a small meadow with a beautiful lakelet and a campsite or two nestled in the whitebark pines on the sandy rise east of the outlet.

After fording that outlet (10,180 — 1.8), you continue descending, this time leveling out on a forested bench by another Lyell Fork crossing (9650 — 1.8), this one with a footbridge. This lovely bench is notable for its many overused, bear-visited campsites. Having crossed the stream, you'll stay on the west bank of the river almost all the way to Tuolumne Meadows. Beyond the bench you make the last major descent — a steep one — down to Lyell Fork base camp (9040 — 1.4), at the southern, upper end of Lyell Canyon. This camp, a moderate trek from Highway 120, is a popular site. Bears scour Lyell Canyon for easy pickings, and hanging your food to protect it is useless on this stretch — bear-resistant canisters are a must! Cables once provided for food-hanging at some Lyell Canyon campsites are being removed because ineffective.

The hike to Highway 120 is now an easy, level, usually open stroll along the meandering Lyell Fork Tuolumne River. Campsites will be found here and there, but camping is permitted only when more than 4 miles from the highway. After crossing Ireland Creek, there's a major camping area at the junction (8901 — 2.8) with a trail to Ireland and Evelyn lakes and Vogelsang High Sierra Camp.

Past the junction, occasional backward glances at receding Potter Point mark your progress north along trout-inhabited Lyell Fork. With the oft-looming threat of afternoon lightning storms, one wishes the trail had been routed along the forest's edge, rather than through open meadow. Typical of meadowy trails, the JMT is multitracked here. Numerous tracks arise mainly because as one main track is used, it gets deepened until it penetrates the near-surface water table and becomes soggy. Odds are great that you'll have to leave the track at least once, thus helping to start a new one.

See Map 23

Shortly after Potter Point finally disappears from view —
and beyond half a dozen campsites — you curve northwest,
descend between two bedrock outcrops, and then contour west
through alternating soggy meadows and lodgepole forests. Both
abound in mosquitoes through late July, as does most of the
Tuolumne Meadows area. Two-branched Rafferty Creek soon
appears, and you cross it on a sturdy footbridge. Just beyond it
you meet the Rafferty Creek Trail (8710 — 4.4), part of the
very scenic and very popular High Sierra Loop Trail — not to
be confused with the trans-range High Sierra Trail far to the
south in Sequoia National Park, whose route you shared from
Whitney's summit to the junction with the trail west down
Wallace Creek.

You continue west and soon meet another junction (8650
— 0.7) and a point of some disagreement. The most recent maps
show, and NPS personnel agree, that to stay on the "official"
JMT, hikers should take the west fork here, toward Tuolumne
Meadows Campground, where hikers may find a few walk-in
sites in this area where camping is otherwise prohibited. However, traditionally, the JMT has taken the north fork here, toward Tuolumne Meadows Lodge and then across Highway 120.
On one point there is no disagreement: services along the highway include a small store, a minimal café, a post office,
Tuolumne Meadows Lodge (showers; reserve any meals or lodging well in advance!), and Tuolumne Meadows Campground.
We'll describe both routes:

Official, current JMT route. Less scenic than the traditional route but avoids Highway 120 altogether. Take the west
(left) fork at the "point of some disagreement" and stroll through
moderate forest, glimpsing Lyell Fork through the trees. You
soon ford an unnamed creek and leave the river behind for an
easy traverse that offers good wildflowers in season. At the next
junction, a trail leads northwest to nearby, popular Tuolumne
Meadows Campground, where hikers may find walk-in sites in
this area where camping is otherwise prohibited. Use trails
radiate to/from the campground, but the JMT continues west
to a junction with the trail from the campground to Elizabeth
Lake and beyond that to a junction with a use trail from the
campground. Continue west, shortly crossing Unicorn Creek
on a footbridge and then fording a small stream. At the next
junction the JMT continues west where another trail comes in

See Maps 23, 24, 25

South to North

The Cathedral Range above Tuolumne Meadows

from the north, from the highway. This is where the official and traditional JMT routes rejoin (8620 — 2.3).

Traditional JMT route. Much more scenic than the official, current route, but requires crossing busy Highway 120 twice. Take the north (right) fork at the "point of some disagreement" and almost immediately cross the Lyell Fork on a pair of bridges spanning the river at an exceptionally pretty spot. A photographing pause here is well worth it, particularly when clouds are building up over Mts. Dana and Gibbs in the northeast. From the bridges, a short, winding climb north followed by an equal descent brings you to Dana Fork Tuolumne River, only 130 yards past a junction with an east-climbing trail to the Gaylor Lakes. Immediately beyond the footbridge, there's a short spur trail (8690 — 0.6) northeast to Tuolumne Meadows Lodge. The JMT parallels Dana Fork downstream, encountering a second spur trail northeast to the lodge. Soon you hear the stream as it makes a small drop into a clear pool, which is almost cut in two by a protruding granite finger. At the base of this finger, about 8 to 10 feet down, is an underwater arch — an extremely rare feature in any kind of rock. If you feel like braving the cold

See Map 24

water, 50° at best, you can dive under and swim through it. Just beyond the pool, you approach the lodge's road (8650 — 0.3), where a short path climbs a few yards up to it and takes one to the entrance of a large parking lot for backpackers.

Continuing on the traditional route, you parallel the paved road westward, passing the Tuolumne Meadows Ranger Station and quickly reaching a junction. The main road curves north to the sometimes-noisy highway, but you follow the spur road west, to where it curves into a second large parking lot for backpackers. In its east end you'll find a booth from which a summer ranger dispenses wilderness permits. The road past the lot becomes a closed dirt road and diminishes to a wide trail by the time you arrive at Highway 120 (8595 — 0.8). The traditional route of the JMT crosses the highway, passes through the parking lot at the foot of massive Lembert Dome, and follows a dirt road 1/2 mile northwest to a gate blocking cars from going farther. It's no barrier to hikers, and you continue northwest along the lodgepole-dotted flank of Tuolumne Meadows, enjoying fine views south across the meadows to Unicorn Peak, Cathedral Peak, and some of the knobby Echo Peaks. Coming to a road fork (8590 — 0.7), you bear left. Nearby to the northwest are Parsons Lodge and McCauley Cabin as well as some rusty-looking, natural soda springs near a tumbledown, roofless shack. A tangle of disused roads, official trails, and use trails makes this area confusing. Your goal is to curve gently southwest and then south through the expansive, well-flowered meadows, crossing the Tuolumne River on a footbridge and then fording a couple of small streams, before cross-

See Maps 24, 25

Soda Springs' tumbledown shack

ing the highway again (8575 — 0.5). Beyond the blacktop you pick up the trail and ascend gently for 300 yards to a junction where the official, current and traditional JMT routes rejoin.

From this junction, the JMT turns west as a wide, dusty trail, and continues west in thick lodgepole forest. Then it crosses rippling Budd Creek on a sturdy bridge and immediately meets the Cathedral Lakes Trail (8570 — 0.9), which began at a parking lot beside the highway (signed CATHEDRAL LAKES) 0.1 mile north of here. Turning southwest onto this trail, you begin a steep but shady climb that in 1/2 mile passes a use trail branching south toward the Budd Lake basin. Your dusty trail levels off presently and descends to a small meadow that is boggy in early season. From here you can see the dramatically shaped tops of Unicorn Peak and The Cockscomb. The apparent granite dome in the south is in reality the north ridge of Cathedral Peak, whose steeples are out of sight over the "dome's" horizon.

Your viewful trail continues to cruise gently up and down through more little meadows set in hemlock forest, and then dips near a tinkling stream whose source, you discover after further walking, is a robust spring on a shady set of switchbacks. Beyond this climb, the tread levels off on the west slope of Cathedral Peak and makes a long, gentle, sparsely forested descent on sandy underfooting to a junction (9460 — 2.7) with the spur trail to lower Cathedral Lake, where camping is currently prohibited — but check the latest regulations. (Not long ago, the lower lake was open to camping and the upper one closed!)

Continue south on the JMT and make an easy mile-long climb to the southeast corner of the shallow bowl cupping upper Cathedral Lake and hemmed in by Cathedral, Echo, and Tressider peaks — a setting of astonishing beauty. If the lake is open to camping, the campsites are few but well worth seeking out on the bowl's gently sloping sides. A photo of two-steepled Cathedral Peak mirrored in the lake's waters, when they are still, will be a treasured souvenir of your JMT journey. The trail then climbs one-fourth mile to Cathedral Pass (9700 — 1.1), a broad saddle that is not the high point on this climb. Excellent views include Tressider Peak, Cathedral Peak, Echo Peaks, Matthes Crest, the Clark Range farther south, and Matterhorn Peak far to the north.

Where the JMT leaves Cathedral Pass climbing gently

See Map 25

Cathedral Peak and lower Cathedral Lake

along the east flank of Tressider Peak, a long, beautiful, trail-less swale, the headwaters of Echo Creek, descends from the pass, offering a display of midseason flowers that's worth the hike from Tuolumne Meadows. The JMT traverses upward to its real high point on this leg (9940′) in 3/4 more mile at a marvelous viewpoint overlooking most of southern Yosemite Park. The inspiring panorama includes the peaks around Vogelsang High Sierra Camp in the southeast, the whole Clark Range in the south, and the peaks on the Park border in both directions

See Maps 25, 26

South to North

farther away. From this viewpoint our high trail then traverses under steep-walled Columbia Finger, then switchbacks quickly down to the head of the upper lobe of Long Meadow, levels off, and leads down a gradually sloping valley dotted with little lodgepole pines to the head of the second, lower lobe of l-o-n-g Long Meadow, whose streams may be dry by late season. After passing a junction (9320 — 2.7) with a trail down Echo Creek, the route levels off and heads south ½ mile before bending west ¼ mile to pass below Sunrise High Sierra Camp (9300 — 0.8), perched on a granite bench just above the trail. South of the camp are some backpacker campsites where you can take in the next morning's glorious sunrise. The JMT angles west below the camp and then angles south again to a junction with a trail northwest to Sunrise Lakes and Clouds Rest. You can take this trail a short distance to find use trails leading to the camp and to the backpacker campsites.

The JMT continues through the south arm of Long Meadow, then soon starts to climb the eastern slopes of Sunrise Mountain. You top a broad, southeast-trending ridge, and then, paralleling the headwaters of Sunrise Creek, descend steeply by switchbacks down a rocky canyon. At the foot of this descent you cross a trickling creek, then climb a low moraine to another creek, and in a short ½ mile top the linear crest of a giant lateral moraine. This moraine is the largest of a series of ridgelike glacial deposits in this area, and the gigantic granite boulders along their sides testify to the power of the glacier that once filled Little Yosemite Valley and its tributary valleys. Most of its rocks have decomposed to soil — an indication of its old age. More morainal crests are identified on both sides of the trail and Half Dome is seen through the trees before our trail reaches a junction (8000 — 5.0) with the Forsyth Trail. There are poor campsites on a rise overlooking Sunrise Creek about 200 yards north of this junction.

Here the JMT turns south and in a moment reaches the High Trail, from Merced and Washburn lakes, coming in on the left. Turning right, you descend southwest, as your path is bounded on the north by giant cliffs — the south buttress of the Clouds Rest eminence — and on the south by Moraine Dome.

A mile from the last junction the JMT fords Sunrise Creek in a red-fir forest whose stillness is broken by the creek's gurgling and by the occasional screams of Steller jays. You soon

See Maps 26, 27

curve northeast to a quck crossing of a tributary which has two west-bank campsites and a large, improved site on the low ridge to the west. Use trails to campsites in this area are so well-worn that you may briefly confuse them with the JMT — but you'll soon discover your error. Immediately past them is a trail to Clouds Rest (7210 — 2.3) and 1/2 mile west from this junction you meet the trail to Half Dome (7015 — 0.5) — about 4 miles round trip and an incredible hike that shouldn't be missed. From this junction your shady path switchbacks down through a changing forest cover that comes to include some stately incense-cedars, with their burnt-orange, fibrous bark, plus sugar and ponderosa pines, white firs, and black oaks. At the foot of this descent a gravelly shortcut trail goes southwest, and its extension northeast ends in 100 yards at some improved campsites on Sunrise Creek. You continue straight ahead (signed backpackers camp) 350 yards across the flat floor of Little Yosemite Valley, past campsites, bear boxes, and toilets, to a junction (6100 — 1.5) with the Merced Lake Trail, not far from the river, which is just out of sight here. A summer ranger usually camps just east of this junction, in the heart of bear country. This is the last camping opportunity before the huge campgrounds of Yosemite Valley.

Turning right in dense forest, you follow the broad trail, which is separated from the banks of the mostly unseen river by a crude log fence, and meet the "shortcut" route in 1/3 mile. The trail ascends almost imperceptibly over a little rise that marks the west end of Little Yosemite Valley. Beyond it, you soon reach a junction with the Mist Trail, which provides a somewhat shorter, more scenic, and steeper route to Happy Isles. Both routes tend to be crowded. In early and mid season, hikers on the Mist Trail must either don rain gear or get soaked to the skin because of the route's proximity to Nevada and Vernal falls — it's not recommended for backpackers! There are toilets located near this junction.

Take the left fork here to stay on the JMT, zigzagging up a little to parallel the river briefly before turning south across polished granite slabs and crossing the river on a footbridge. Here the Merced River takes its mightiest plunge — 594 feet over Nevada Fall. The view from the brink of the fall is unforgettable — the cauldron of flying water stands in stark relief to the serenity of the trail, and the barren solidity of Liberty Cap is a reassuring reminder of the solid rock on which the viewer stands.

See Map 27

The trail may be hard to spot on the other side of the bridge, but just head into the forest, and you'll find it. Use trails dart off here and there, but stick to the well-worn JMT. About 300 yards beyond the fall, the Panorama Trail (5950 — 1.4) departs southward, bound for Glacier Point, and the JMT begins to follow a paved, walled-in section that clings to the side of a very steep granite slope. Then it switchbacks down to Clark Point (5481 — 1.0), where there are fine views of the deep canyon of the Merced River and Nevada Fall. From here a lateral trail, the Clark Trail, descends rocky switchbacks to meet the Mist Trail a little upstream of Vernal Fall.

From Clark Point the JMT descends steeply by a score of switchbacks on a part-dirt, part-asphalt tread. Near the bottom of the switchbacks the JMT passes in quick succession a junction with a signed HORSE TRAIL, a junction with the lower end of the Mist Trail, restrooms, and a drinking fountain just before a wooden bridge (4520 — 1.1) that crosses the Merced and provides a superb view of Vernal Fall. Millions of photos of the fall have been taken from here, and you'll want to take one, too. Then the trail rises briefly onto the steep north canyon wall, curves down around Sierra Point while staying high above the cascading river, and finally descends past minor trail junctions to the end of the JMT by a stream-gaging station at Happy Isles (4035 — 0.9), by a sign indicating that this is the northern terminus of the JMT.

You've made it — congratulations!

To get the rest of the way into Yosemite Valley, cross the bridge by the stream-gaging station and turn right on the second paved path you meet, past restrooms, to the stop for the free Yosemite Valley shuttlebus. Or you can hike one last mile to Camp Curry and pick up the shuttlebus there. Lodgings and campsites in the Valley are in high demand; if you want to spend the night in the Valley, make arrangements well in advance. The shuttlebus serves all of the Valley's lodgings and most of the campgrounds except the unreserved Sunnyside Walk-in Campground.

If you are being picked up by friends, know that if the plan to eliminate most private vehicles from the Valley has taken effect, you may need to take a for-fee bus to a gateway point outside the Valley to meet your friends. Be sure you and your friends clearly understand in advance where, when, and how you can meet!

South to North

See Maps 27, 28

Appendix A.
Trail Profile

Trail profiles help you see trail distance and steepness at a glance. On the following two pages is a profile for the JMT, including the Mt. Whitney Trail to Whitney Portal.

In these profiles the vertical scale is greatly exaggerated. Nevertheless, the steepness of the slopes on these profiles is related to how you feel when you have to carry a pack up them!

Note that horizontal distance is measured along the horizontal axis, not along the profile line. Hence, the steeper a line segment, the more the distance along it will exceed the actual distance between the points it connects.

The profile data are based on work by James Bodmer, copyright © 1994, and used by kind permission.

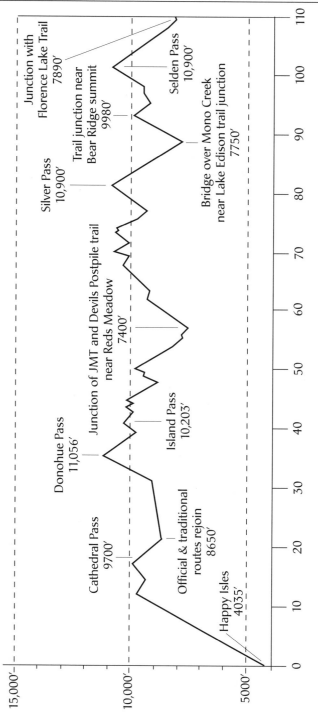

Junction with
Florence Lake Trail
7890'

Selden Pass
10,900'

Trail junction near
Bear Ridge summit
9980'

Silver Pass
10,900'

Bridge over Mono Creek
near Lake Edison trail junction
7750'

Junction of JMT and Devils Postpile trail
near Reds Meadow
7400'

Donohue Pass
11,056'

Island Pass
10,203'

Cathedral Pass
9700'

Official & traditional
routes rejoin
8650'

Happy Isles
4035'

15,000'

10,000'

5000'

0   10   20   30   40   50   60   70   80   90   100   110

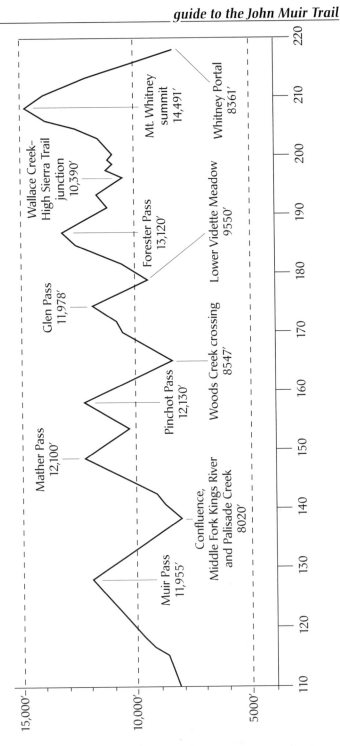

Muir Pass 11,955'

Confluence, Middle Fork Kings River and Palisade Creek 8020'

Mather Pass 12,100'

Pinchot Pass 12,130'

Woods Creek crossing 8547'

Glen Pass 11,978'

Forester Pass 13,120'

Lower Vidette Meadow 9550'

Wallace Creek–High Sierra Trail junction 10,390'

Mt. Whitney summit 14,491'

Whitney Portal 8361'

Appendix B
Getting On and Off the JMT
and Resupply Options

You need to know where and how to get on and off the JMT in order to break your trip into segments, to bail out if the weather turns bad or you get sick, to get back on when the weather improves or you get well, or to resupply. In the following paragraphs, we'll list your on/off options from north to south, telling you:

- Junction's description and elevation.
- Whether we recommend a place for on/off and resupply. A "Not recommended" rating may reflect a needlessly long hike out, a too-rugged route, and/or a trailhead lacking in and distant from any amenities like lodgings, campgrounds, restaurants, and stores.
- Topos covering the on/off routes, especially if the route isn't covered by the maps in this book. "WILD" means it's a Wilderness Press-published 15' topo; otherwise, it's a USGS 7½' topo.
- Agency in whose jurisdiction the trailhead is, if you need to get a permit (see "Wilderness Permits" in the "Introduction"). Abbreviations: YNP = Yosemite National Park; SiNF = Sierra National Forest; INF = Inyo National Forest; SEKI = Sequoia and Kings Canyon National Parks.
- The junction's distance (**Location**) from the terminuses of the JMT, Happy Isles in Yosemite Valley in the north (abbreviated "YV") and Whitney Portal in the south (abbreviated "WP"). Yes, the *official* southern terminus of the JMT is Mt. Whitney's summit at 14,491 feet, but that's an impractical place to end your trip! We'll abbreviate "mile(s)" as "mi." *Note that all distances from Whitney Portal include the 3.8-mi. out-and-back distance to/from Whitney's summit.*
- Whether you exit to the east or the west side of the Sierra. For all practical purposes, towns where you can resupply are on the east side, though there are resorts on the west side that provide package-drops and, sometimes, small stores. East-side towns are connected to the rest of the

world by daily commercial bus service (Greyhound) between Reno, Nevada, and Los Angeles, California.

- Amount of hiking involved and camping opportunities along the way, if it's a long hike, described from the JMT *out* to a trailhead. Reverse the steps if you're going *in*. Unless otherwise specified, assume it's a one-day hike or less.
- Amenities you'll find at the trailheads and in nearby communities, if any.
- Options, if any, for receiving resupply packages. Assume that any place having a post office can hold properly-sent resupply packages for you for a limited time (see **Supplies** in this book's **Introduction**).
- How to get to the trailhead.

This section doesn't include cross-country routes (e.g., Italy Pass) or routes we think are impractical (e.g., the High Sierra Trail). Most of the route and trailhead information is drawn from other Wilderness Press books, mainly *Sierra North*, *Sierra South*, and *Hot Showers, Soft Beds, and Dayhikes in the Sierra*. Consult those volumes, especially the first two, for greater detail about these routes.

Near the end of this appendix, you'll find information on mailing resupply packages to two resorts and to post offices.

Happy Isles (4035'). Recommended

Maps: WILD Yosemite; USGS Half Dome.
Permits: YNP.
Location: 0 mi. from YV, 218.3 mi. from WP.
Exit to: West side.
The hike: None required.
At the trailhead: toilets, water, nature center, snack bar (when rebuilt). Access via free, seasonal shuttlebus to all Yosemite Valley amenities (restaurants, lodging, stores, campgrounds, post office). Some amenities seasonal. Official northern terminus of the JMT.
How to get to the trailhead: In Yosemite Valley, take the shuttlebus to the Happy Isles stop, or hike 1 mile southeast from Camp Curry.

Tuolumne Meadows (8575'–8595'). Recommended.

Maps: WILD Tuolumne Meadows; USGS Tenaya Lake, Tioga Pass, Vogelsang Peak.

Permits: YNP.

Location: Between 21.0 and 24.2 mi. from YV, 194.1 and 197.3 mi. from WP. See below for trailheads.

Exit to: West side, but even easier access to east-side town of Lee Vining (below).

The hike: Almost none; see below for trailheads.

At the trailheads: The trailheads have no amenities right at them, except the pit toilets at Lembert Dome, but nearby are a visitor center, a small store, and a minimal café, and showers at the lodge (but reservations for lodging and/or meals should be made well in advance).

Some hikers consider Tuolumne Meadows an alternate northern terminus of the JMT if they can't get permits to start at Happy Isles or want to avoid the initial climb out of Yosemite Valley.

Access points along a 2-mile stretch of State Route 120 (Tioga Road) in Tuolumne Meadows:

- *Cathedral Lakes Trailhead* is near the Tuolumne Meadows visitor center; this is where you'll meet Tuolumne Meadows if you are hiking the JMT from Yosemite Valley. It's 0.1 mile from 120 to the JMT. **How to get to the trailhead**: The signed CATHEDRAL LAKES trailhead is 8.3 mi. southwest of Tioga Pass on 120.

- *Lembert Dome.* The traditional route of the JMT crosses 120 to the Lembert Dome parking lot. **How to get to the trailhead**: The huge dome and the parking lot at its foot are 7 mi. southwest of Tioga Pass.

- *Backpackers' parking lot trailhead* is at Tuolumne Meadows Wilderness Permit Station, on a paved spur road off 120 to Tuolumne Meadows Lodge, and the traditional route passes very near this lot. **How to get to the trailhead**: The signed TUOLUMNE LODGE turnoff is about 6 1/2 mi. southwest of Tioga Pass; turn here and go a short way down the turnoff, then hard right onto a spur and into the parking lot.

Lee Vining. Small town with lodging, restaurants, groceries, stores, post office (zip: 93541).

Junction with Rush Creek Trail (9600'). Recommended

Maps: USGS Mt. Ritter, Koip Peak.
Permits: INF.

Location: 40.9 mi. from YV, 177.4 mi. from WP.

Exit to: East side.

The hike: Allow 1–2 days. Access to June Lake (below). Go 10.3 mi. east on Rush Creek Trail to Silver Lake on State Route 158. No major passes to cross; campsites along the way.

At the trailhead: seasonal ranger kiosk, toilet. Nearby: campground, Silver Lake Resort.

How to get to the trailhead: From the southern junction of US Highway 395 with State Route 158, drive southwest for 7.2 mi. through June Lake village, past June Mountain Ski Area, and just past Silver Lake Resort to a large parking lot west of the road.

June Lake. Small town with lodging, restaurants, groceries, stores, post office (zip: 93529).

Junction with Shadow Lake Trail to Agnew Meadows (8750'). Recommended

Maps: WILD Devils Postpile; USGS Mt. Ritter, Mammoth Mtn.

Permits: INF.

Location: 49.7 mi. from YV, 168.6 mi. from WP.

Exit to: East side.

The hike: Go 3.5 mi. east past Shadow Lake to Agnew Meadows, then 1/4 mile on a dirt spur road to find Devils Postpile Road and a stop for seasonal shuttlebus service (hefty fee) to Mammoth Mountain Ski Area/Bike Park.

At the trailhead: toilets, nearby pack station. Access to Mammoth Lakes (below).

How to get to the trailhead: At the junction of US Highway 395 and State Route 203, turn west through the town of Mammoth Lakes to the intersection where 203 turns right, toward Mammoth Mountain Ski Area and Devils Postpile. *Zero your odometer at this intersection.* Turn right and follow 203 at least as far as the ski area, where, in summer during the day, you may be obliged to park and take a for-hefty-fee shuttlebus down into the Postpile area. Before 7:30 AM and after 5:30 PM you may be able to continue driving your own car. Let's assume the latter, so you continue up over Minaret Summit and begin descending a steep, one-lane road. At a hairpin turn, turn right on a dirt road and go past Agnew Meadows Pack Station to either of two parking lots, 8.4–8.5 mi. The trailhead is on the south side of the first of the two lots.

Mammoth Lakes. Small town – but Eastern Sierra's largest – with ample lodging, restaurants, grocery stores, mountaineering and sporting-goods stores, post office (zip: 93546). Ranks with Bishop (below) as your best choice if you must go out to a town to resupply.

Junction with trail to Devils Postpile (7677'). Recommended

Maps: WILD Devils Postpile; USGS Mammoth Mtn.
Permits: INF.
Location: About 55.8 mi. from YV, 162.5 mi. from WP.
Exit to: East side.
The hike: Go 3/4 mi. southeast to Middle Fork San Joaquin River opposite Devils Postpile. Cross bridge over river and go left at next junction a short distance to visitor center and a stop for seasonal shuttlebus service (hefty fee) to Mammoth Mountain Ski Area/Bike Park (above).
At the trailhead: toilets, water, usually-jammed campground, visitor center. Access to Mammoth Lakes (also above). Nearby: several campgrounds.
How to get to the trailhead: Follow the directions above to Agnew Meadows as far as the hairpin turn; don't turn here, but continue on the paved road to the signed turnoff for Devils Postpile. Turn right here and soon come to a crowded parking lot, 12.6 mi.

Junction with trail to Rainbow Falls Trailhead, Reds Meadow (7600'). Recommended

Maps: WILD Devils Postpile; USGS Crystal Crag.
Permits: INF.
Location: 57.6 mi. from YV, 160.7 mi. from WP.
Exit to: East side.
The hike: Go 1/2 mi. north to trailhead and a stop for seasonal shuttlebus service (hefty fee) to Mammoth Mountain Ski Area/Bike Park (above). Access to Mammoth Lakes (above).
At the trailhead: toilet, water. Nearby: Reds Meadow Resort (seasonal lodging, café, store); Reds Meadow Campground (free, hot-spring-fed showers). In the half-mile or so south of this junction, several use/spur trails lead north to Reds Meadow Resort. Also nearby: several campgrounds.
How to get to the trailhead: Follow the directions to Devils Postpile as far as the turnoff to Devils Postpile but don't turn; instead, continue on the road to a Y-junction where left is a paved road to Reds Meadow Resort, right is a dirt road

to a parking lot for Rainbow Falls, 13.7 mi.

Junction with trail to Mammoth Pass in lower Crater Meadow (8700'). Recommended

Maps: WILD Devils Postpile; USGS Crystal Crag.
Permits: INF.
Location: 61.2 mi. from YV, 157.1 mi. from WP.
Exit to: East side.
The hike: Go east along Crater Meadow and then briefly west to a junction with a shortcut to Upper Crater Meadow (and a former route of the JMT). In a few more steps there's another junction with a trail going west and north to Reds Meadow. You curve north, presently passing a junction near a noisy spring with the trail from Upper Crater Meadow (below). Continue north, then east, over forested Mammoth Pass (9350'), to McCloud Lake, near the east end of which you find a junction with a trail going northwest. You go ahead, east and northeast, to the trailhead at Horseshoe Lake, a total hike of 3 1/2 miles.
At the trailhead: toilets. Nearby: you are in a lakes basin southwest of Mammoth Lakes, and there are campgrounds, lodgings, and a few stores widely scattered along the roads through the basin. Access to Mammoth Lakes (above).
How to get to the trailhead: At the junction of US Highway 395 and State Route 203, turn west through the town of Mammoth Lakes to the intersection where 203 turns right, toward Mammoth Mountain Ski Area and Devils Postpile. *Zero your odometer at this intersection.* Continue ahead, now on the Lake Mary Road, and follow it past a turnoff to Twin Lakes, past the Mammoth Pack Station, to a Y-junction where it's left to skirt Lake Mary's east shore, right to skirt Lake Mary's north shore and then go to Lake Mamie and Horseshoe Lake. Turn right and soon pass a road turning left toward Lake George; you go straight here, all the way to the road's end at Horseshoe Lake, about 5.7 mi.

Junction with trail to Mammoth Pass in Upper Crater Meadow (8890'). Recommended

Maps: WILD Devils Postpile; USGS Crystal Crag.
Permits: INF.
Location: 62.1 mi. from YV, 156.2 mi. from WP.
Exit to: East side.

The hike: Go north on rolling terrain to meet the trail from lower Crater Meadow in 1 1/4 mi. Continue over Mammoth Pass as described for **Junction with trail to Mammoth Pass in lower Crater Meadow**, above, for a total hike of not quite 3 mi. Access to Mammoth Lakes (above).

How to get to the trailhead: See above for Horseshoe Lake.

Junction with Duck Pass Trail (10,150'). Recommended

Maps: USGS Bloody Mtn.
Permits: INF.
Location: 70.1 mi. from YV, 148.2 mi. from WP.
Exit to: East side.
The hike: Allow 1–2 days. Go 6 mi. over Duck Pass (10,797'; snow likely on north side) to Coldwater Canyon Trailhead. Campsites along the way; no camping within 300 feet of Duck Lake's outlet.
At the trailhead: toilets, water, campground. Nearby: as for Mammoth Pass, above. Access to Mammoth Lakes (above).
How to get to the trailhead: At the junction of US Highway 395 and State Route 203, turn west through the town of Mammoth Lakes to the point where 203 turns right, toward Mammoth Mountain Ski Area and Devils Postpile. *Zero your odometer at this intersection.* Continue ahead, now on the Lake Mary Road, and follow it past a turnoff to Twin Lakes, past the Mammoth Pack Station, to a Y-junction where it's left to skirt Lake Mary's east shore, right to skirt Lake Mary's north shore. Turn left here, past Pine City Campground, around Lake Mary to a spur road into Coldwater Campground near the south end of the lake. Turn left into Coldwater Campground and follow signs on the mostly-one-way roads to a large parking lot at the top of Coldwater Campground, 5.2 mi. There are three trailheads here; the Duck Pass Trailhead is the middle one.

Junction with McGee Pass Trail at Tully Hole (9520'). Not recommended

Maps: USGS Bloody Mtn., Graveyard Peak, Mt. Abbott, Convict Lake.
Permits: INF.
Location: 76.4 mi. from YV, 141.9 mi. from WP.
Exit to: East side.
The hike: Go 15.5 tough mi. up Fish Creek and over rugged

McGee Pass (11,909'; snow likely on east side) to McGee Creek
Trailhead. Allow 2–3 days. Campsites along the way.

At the trailhead: toilet. Nearby: campground, pack station down
the road. Catch a ride to Mammoth Lakes (above).

How to get to the trailhead: From US Highway 395 between
Bishop and Mammoth Lakes, turn southwest on signed
McGee Canyon Road and follow it 3.2 mi. past McGee Pack
Station to a roadend parking loop.

Junction with Mono Pass Trail (8270'). Not recommended

Maps: USGS Graveyard Peak, Mt. Abbot, Mt. Morgan.
Permits: INF.
Location: 86.6 mi. from YV, 131.7 mi. from WP.
Exit to: East side.
The hike: Allow 2–3 days. Go about 15.1 arduous mi. up Mono
Creek and over steep Mono Pass (12,000') to Mosquito Flat
Trailhead. Campsites along the way.

At the trailhead: toilets. Nearby: campgrounds, lodgings (cafés,
stores) down Rock Creek Road. Catch a ride to Mammoth
Lakes (see above) or Bishop (see below).

How to get to the trailhead: From US Highway 395, turn west
on Rock Creek Road at Toms Place and follow the road *past*
Rock Creek Lake, beyond the turnoff for which the road
shortly becomes one lane. Continue all the way to the roadend
parking lot, 9.2 mi.

*Bishop. Small town – but Eastern Sierra's second largest. Ample
lodging, restaurants, grocery stores, mountaineering and sporting-
goods stores, post office (zip: 93514). Ranks with Mammoth Lakes
(above) as your best choice if you must go out to a town to resupply.*

Junction with Lake Edison trail (7750'). Recommended

Maps: USGS Graveyard Peak, Sharktooth Peak.
Permits: SiNF.
Location: About 88.2 mi. from YV, 130.1 mi. from WP.
Exit to: West side.
The hike: Go southwest 1 mile to a junction with a spur trail to
a landing for twice-daily ferry service (seasonal; fee) across
Lake Edison to Vermilion Valley Resort at the lake's west
end, or 4 1/2 trail mi. to the trailhead at Vermilion Camp-
ground near the lake's west end.

At the trailhead: campground, water, toilets. Nearby: seasonal

Vermilion Valley Resort (see **Seasonal resorts near the JMT** near the end of this appendix). In drought years, Lake Edison is drained till little is left but mud, and the resort closes and ferry service ends earlier than usual, which is the end of the fishing season. Farther away down access road: Mono Hot Springs Resort (store, lodging, hot-spring-fed baths, café, post office; summer, write General Delivery, Mono Hot Springs, CA 93642, or phone (209) 325-1710; winter, write P.O. Box 215, Lakeshore, CA 93634, same phone.) To mail a resupply package to the post office at Mono Hot Springs Resort, see **Mailing a resupply package to a post office** near the end of this appendix. No nearby towns.

How to get to the trailhead: The hike to the trailhead is okay, but the drive to the trailhead is a major undertaking. Take State Route 168 through Clovis and up into the foothills, through the community of Shaver Lake. The state route officially ends at a turnoff to Huntington Lake and its little community, Lakeshore, but you continue ahead on what is now Kaiser Pass Road. The road shortly becomes narrow and twisting, and at Kaiser Pass becomes even more narrow and twisting — add steep and in poor repair, too — before making an airy, tortuous descent past the High Sierra Ranger Station (seasonal) to a **Y**-junction where it's left to Mono Hot Springs Resort, Lake Edison, and Vermilion Valley Resort, right to Florence Lake. Turn left, past the turnoffs to Mono Hot Springs and Vermilion Valley resorts, as the road turns to dirt. Pass the first turnoff for Vermilion Campground, pass the pack station turnoff, and follow the road through the campground to the farthest end of the farthest-east campground loop, where there's a parking area bounded by huge logs, 89+ mi. from Clovis.

Junction with trail on Bear Ridge to road by Lake Edison dam (9980′). Not recommended

No current information. Prefer the Lake Edison Trail, the trail to Bear Diversion Dam, or the Florence Lake Trail.

Junction with trail down Bear Creek to Bear Diversion Dam (9040′). Recommended

Maps: WILD Mt. Abbott; USGS Florence Lake, Mt. Givens.
Permits: SiNF.
Location: 94.4 mi. from YV, 123.9 mi. from WP.

Exit to: West side.

The hike: Go southwest down Bear Creek 9 mi., the last 2.5 mi. from Bear Diversion Dam on an OHV road, to the road linking Lake Edison with the rest of the world. Campsites along the way. Access to Mono Hot Springs — nearer, about 1 mile south on the regular road and then a short distance down a signed spur road) and Vermilion Valley resorts, and several campgrounds.

How to get to the trailhead: Refer to the driving directions to Lake Edison. Turn left at the **Y**-junction as for Lake Edison, but in 2.5 mi. find Bear Diversion Dam road junction (with an OHV route) on your right, about 83.5 mi. from Clovis. Passenger cars can't go beyond here; the OHV route goes 2.5 more mi. to Bear Diversion Dam, and high-clearance 4WD vehicles may be able to make it.

Junctions with Florence Lake Trail past Muir Trail Ranch. *Recommended*

Maps: USGS Florence Lake, Ward Mountain. Note that those USGS topos are *not* currently accurate regarding these junctions.

Permits: SiNF.

Location: See below.

Exit to: West side.

The hike: Two junctions:

- *Northern access:* 8400′. 107.4 mi. from YV, 110.9 mi. from WP. Southbound hikers can take a lateral trail on their way down from Senger Creek and descend to the Florence Lake Trail in less than a mile; Muir Trail Ranch is about 1/4 mile more west.

- *Southern access*: 7890′. 109.1 mi. from YV, 109.2 mi. from WP. Northbound hikers should take the Florence Lake Trail at the junction 1.8 mi. beyond the junction with the Piute Pass Trail. Go west 1 1/2 mi. to Muir Trail Ranch (package drop; see **Seasonal resorts near the JMT** near the end of this appendix). Campsites nearby. Across the South Fork San Joaquin River are a hot pool, part of Blayney Hot Springs, and a warmish lake (campsites on both sides of the river). Or continue 5 more mi. to spur trail to landing for ferry service (fee) across Florence Lake to trailhead. Or continue hiking 5 more mi. (10 total) around the lake to the trailhead. Campsites

along the way. In drought years Florence Lake, like Lake
Edison, may be drained till it's not much more than mud,
and ferry service may end earlier than usual, which is
the end of the fishing season.

At the trailhead: toilets, water, adjacent Florence Lake Store.
Farther down the road are campgrounds, seasonal Vermilion Valley Resort, and Mono Hot Springs Resort; see above
for "Lake Edison." No nearby towns.

How to get to the trailhead: Follow the above directions over
Kaiser Pass as far as the Y-junction and turn right to Florence Lake. Follow this very poor, very narrow road to the
roadend parking area, about 87 mi. from Clovis.

Junction with Piute Creek Trail (8050'). Not recommended
unless you need to exit to a town, because nearby Muir Trail Ranch (see
above) is a package drop.

Maps: WILD Mt. Goddard; USGS Mt. Hilgard, Mt. Darwin, Mt.
Thompson.

Permits: INF.

Location: 110.9 mi. from YV, 107.4 mi. from WP.

Exit to: East side.

The hike: Allow 3 days. Go northeast about 4.6 mi. to a junction
at Hutchinson Meadow; few campsites along the way. Then
continue either:

- *Northeast* 13 more mi. through French Canyon over Pine
Creek Pass (11,100') to Pine Creek Trailhead. Campsites
along the way. **At the trailhead:** pack station. Access to
Bishop (above). **How to get to the trailhead:** At the junction of US Highway 395 and the signed road to Rovana,
go 10 mi. west through Rovana to a signed parking area
beside Pine Creek.

- *East* 11 more mi. through Humphreys Basin over Piute
Pass (11,423') to North Lake Campground. Campsites
along the way. **At the trailhead:** campground, toilet, water.
Nearby: down the road, pack station, Cardinal Village
Resort (lodging, café, store), campgrounds. Access to Bishop
(above). **How to get to the trailhead:** From the junction of
US Highway 395 and State Route 168 (West Line Street)
in Bishop, go southwest 18 mi., almost to Lake Sabrina,
but just before that lake, turn right onto a some-spots-airy
dirt road to North Lake. Go 2 mi. to a backpacker's parking area just beyond North Lake and next to the pack sta-

tion. The trailhead is 1/2 mi. more mile ahead, in the North Lake Campground, but you can't park there.

Junction with Bishop Pass Trail (8710'). Recommended

Maps: WILD Mt. Goddard; USGS North Palisade, Mt. Thompson.
Permits: INF.
Location: 134.7 mi. from YV, 83.6 mi. from WP.
Exit to: East side.
The hike: Allow 2 days. Go east about 11.6 steep mi. out of Le Conte Canyon, through Dusy Basin, and over Bishop Pass (11,972') to South Lake trailhead. Campsites along the way.
At the trailhead: toilets, water. Nearby: down the road, pack station, Parchers Resort, and Bishop Creek Lodge (lodgings, cafés, stores), campgrounds. Access to Bishop (above).
How to get to the trailhead: From the junction of US Highway 395 and State Route 168 (West Line Street) in Bishop, go southwest 15 1/2 mi. to a fork, where you turn left and go 7 more mi. to parking at South Lake.

Junction with Taboose Pass Trail (10,794'). Not recommended

Maps: WILD Mt. Pinchot; USGS Mt. Pinchot, Aberdeen.
Permits: INF.
Location: 154.7 mi. from YV, 63.6 mi. from WP.
Exit to: East side.
The hike: Junction may be unsigned. Allow 2–3 days. Go 11 mi. on poor trail over Taboose Pass (11,418') to make a horrendous descent on miserable footing to Taboose Creek Roadend. Few campsites along the way.
At the trailhead: no amenities. Access to Big Pine (below).
How to get to the trailhead: Turn west on a dirt road that leaves US Highway 395 12 mi. south of Big Pine or 15 mi. north of Independence. Go right at a fork at 1.7 more mi., pass through a gate at 2.4 mi., and continue to the roadend at 5.8 mi. The last 1/4 mile is very rough.

Big Pine: Small town with lodging, cafés, stores, post office (zip: 93513).

Junction with Sawmill Pass Trail (10,347'). Not recommended

Maps: WILD Mt. Pinchot; USGS Mt. Pinchot, Aberdeen.
Permits: INF.
Location: 161.5 mi. from YV, 56.8 mi. from WP.

Exit to: East side.

The hike: Junction may be unsigned. Allow 2–3 days. Go 13½
total mi. east on a faint, steep, often overgrown trail into a
lakes basin with almost no campsites, then over Sawmill
Pass (11,347') to make a very steep descent with a few campsites to Sawmill Creek Roadend. Hot, dusty lower reaches
partly overgrown by leg-slashing shrubs.

At the trailhead: no amenities. Access to Big Pine (above) and
Independence (below).

How to get to the trailhead: Turn west on a dirt road signed
BLACK ROCK SPRINGS ROAD that leaves US Highway 395 17.5
mi. south of Big Pine or 9.5 miles north of Independence. Go
west 0.8 more mile to a junction. Turn north and follow Old
US 395 1.2 mi. to Division Creek Road, leading west. Follow
this road 2.1 mi. to the trailhead.

*Independence: Small town with lodgings, cafés, groceries, stores,
post office (zip: 93526).*

Junction with Woods Creek Trail (8547'). Recommended

Maps: USGS Mt. Clarence King, The Sphinx.
Permits: SEKI.
Location: 165.4 mi. from YV, 52.9 mi. from WP.
Exit to: West side.
The hike: Allow 2 days. Go 14 mi. southwest through Paradise
Valley to Cedar Grove Roadend (5035') in Kings Canyon.
Campsites, bear boxes on the way; no camping below Para-
dise Valley.

At the trailhead: no amenities. Nearby: National Park Service
(NPS) facility at Cedar Grove (lodging, café, limited store,
campgrounds). No nearby towns.

How to get to the trailhead: Go 85 mi. east from Fresno on State
Route 180 past Grant Grove Village in Kings Canyon National
Park (park headquarters is located here), over a summit, then
down into Kings Canyon to Cedar Grove Roadend, 6 mi. east of
Cedar Grove Village (also a national-park village).

Junction with Baxter Pass Trail (10,230'). Not recommended

Maps: WILD Mt. Pinchot; USGS Mt. Clarence King, Kearsarge
Peak.
Permits: INF.
Location: 169.1 mi. from YV, 49.2 mi. from WP.

Exit to: East side.

The hike: Junction may be unsigned. Allow 2-3 days. Go 13.3 mi. first through Baxter Lakes basin (campsites), then over Baxter Pass (12,320′) to descend a rough trail with a few campsites to Oak Creek Roadend.

At the trailhead: no amenities. Nearby: campground down the road. Access to Independence (above).

How to get to the trailhead: Turn west from US Highway 395 2.3 mi. north of Independence onto paved Fish Hatchery Road and go 1.3 more mi. to a junction. Go right here, passing Oak Creek Campground, to Oak Creek Roadend parking lot 5.8 more mi.

Junctions with Kearsarge Pass Trail. Recommended

Maps: WILD Mt. Pinchot; USGS Mt. Clarence King, Kearsarge Peak.

Permits: INF.

Location: See below.

Exit to: East side.

The hike: Allow 1–2 days. 3 junctions close together, between Glen Pass and Vidette Meadow.

- *North* (10,826′): About 176.6 mi. from YV, 41.7 mi. from WP. Go 7 mi. on a long, dry traverse without campsites, unless you detour to Kearsarge Lakes (campsites, bear boxes), then over Kearsarge Pass (11,823′) through an east-side lakes basin (ghastly bear problems) to Onion Valley Trailhead (9200′).
- *Middle* (10,710′): 176.8 mi. from YV, 41.5 mi. from WP. A spur trail branching from X-junction with trail to Charlotte Lake that shortly intersects the trail from the north junction, above.
- *South* (10,530′): 177.5 mi. from YV, 40.8 mi. from WP. Go about 7 mi. up through the Bullfrog-Kearsarge Basin to Kearsarge Lakes (campsites, bear boxes), then climb steeply to meet the trail from the north junction a little west of Kearsarge Pass (see above). Bullfrog Lake is closed to camping.

At the trailhead: toilet, water, campground. Access to Independence (above).

How to get to the trailhead: At the junction of US Highway 395 and Market Street in Independence, turn west on Market Street (Onion Valley Road) and follow it for 13 1/3 steep, winding mi. to a large parking area that serves three trailheads; Kearsarge Pass is the middle trailhead.

Junction with Bubbs Creek Trail to Cedar Grove Roadend (9950'). Recommended

Maps: USGS Mt. Clarence King, The Sphinx.
Permits: SEKI.
Location: 179 mi. from YV, 39.3 mi. to WP.
Exit to: West side.
The hike: Allow 1–2 days. Go about 13 mi. west, mostly along Bubbs Creek, to Cedar Grove Roadend (see above for **Junction with Woods Creek Trail**). Campsites, bear boxes along the way.

Junction with Shepherd Pass Trail (10,930'). Not recommended

Maps: WILD Mt. Whitney; USGS Mt. Williamson.
Permits: INF.
Location: 192 mi. from YV, 26.3 mi. from WP.
Exit to: East side.
The hike: Junction may be unsigned. Allow 2 days. Go 12.7 mi. over Shepherd Pass (12,050'; snow may linger on the east side) to make a miserable descent with some campsites, to Symmes Creek Trailhead.
At the trailhead: no amenities. Access to Independence (above).
How to get to the trailhead: From US Highway 395 go 4½ mi. west on Market Street (Onion Valley Road) to Foothill Road. Turn left on Foothill Road and go 1.3 mi. to a fork. Take the right-hand fork and go past an old corral on the left, then immediately cross Symmes Creek. In ½ mile take the right fork, and take the right fork again at the next two forks. Then go ½ to the trailhead near Symmes Creek. Some of these forks may have small signs.

Junction with trail over Mt. Whitney (10,880') and with southbound Pacific Crest Trail (PCT) to Horseshoe Meadow

Maps: WILD Mt. Whitney; USGS Mt. Whitney, Mt. Langley, Cirque Peak.
Permits: INF.
Location: 199.8 mi. from YV, 18.5 mi. from WP.
Exit to: East side.
The hike: Allow 3 days.

 • _Over Mt. Whitney:_ A qualified "recommended" only be-

cause the ascent of Whitney *is* the JMT's route. Depend-
ing on whether you're going to the JMT or from the JMT,
follow the start of the **South-to-North** chapter or the end
of the **North-to-South** chapter in this book. **At the trailhead**: store, café, water, toilets, campground. Nearby:
campgrounds down the road. Access to Lone Pine (below). **How to get to the trailhead**: From US Highway 395
in Lone Pine, go 13 mi. west on Whitney Portal Road.
There are two parking lots on different levels.

- *Southbound PCT to Horseshoe Meadow:* A qualified "recommended" as an alternate southern access to the JMT
(sometimes called "Whitney South") when you can't get
a permit for Whitney Portal. Not recommended as an
exit from the JMT. Go about 21 mi. on the PCT across
Guyot Flat, then over a saddle (10,925') east of Mount
Guyot; descend to Rock Creek; then ascend past Chicken
Spring Lake to a junction with the trail over Cottonwood
Pass (11,200') to the trailhead at Horseshoe Meadow.
Campsites, some with bear boxes, along the way. **At the
trailhead**: toilet, water, campground, nearby pack station.
Access to Lone Pine (below). **How to get to the trailhead**:
From US Highway 395 in Lone Pine, go 3.5 mi. west on
Whitney Portal Road, turn left, and go 20½ mi. on Horse-
shoe Meadow Road, past the turnoff to Cottonwood Lakes
Trailhead, to a large parking lot at the roadend.

Lone Pine: *Small town with lodgings, restaurants, groceries,
stores, post office (zip: 93545).*

Seasonal resorts near the JMT

As mentioned in the **Introduction**, two seasonal resorts
near JMT junctions will, for a fee, hold resupply packages for
you. *Be sure to write them well in advance to learn their fees
and package-drop policies; include a stamped, self-addressed
envelope for their replies!*

Vermilion Valley Resort

See **Junction with Lake Edison trail** (7750'), above. The resort offers lodging, camping, café, and a store. They accept package drops. Vermilion Valley Resort has recently become very
hospitable to JMT and PCT travelers. A visit there will be a
highlight of your trip. They have an e-mail address, but no one
seems to answer their e-mail. Write or call —

Vermilion Valley Resort
P.O. Box 258
Lakeshore, CA 93634
(209) 259-4000 (seasonal, at the resort)
(209) 855-6558 (office)
Web site: http://www.edisonlake.com

Muir Trail Ranch

See **Junctions with Florence Lake Trail past Muir Trail Ranch,** above. Muir Trail Ranch offers only package-drop service for hikers; its lodgings and food are reserved for its own guests, who stay by the week. However, there are campsites nearby and a free hot-spring pool across the river (the ford may be very dangerous in early season). Write or call —

Muir Trail Ranch
Spring / summer address:
Box 176
Lakeshore, CA 93634
(no phone at resort)
Autumn / winter address:
P.O. Box 269
Ahwahnee, CA 93601
(209) 966-3195

Mailing a resupply package to a post office

Post offices will be found in all the east-side towns reasonably accessible from the JMT. See above for details of getting to/from the towns.

A reasonably accessible post office is on the west side of the range at Mono Hot Springs Resort, CA 93642. From the following JMT junctions, you can walk to the road that Mono Hot Springs is 1/4 mile west of, on a spur road: **Junction with Lake Edison trail (7750′) and Junction with trail down Bear Creek to Bear Diversion Dam (9040′).**

When mailing your package to any of these places, address it to:

[Yourself]
General Delivery
P.O., CA [zip]
HOLD UNTIL [date]

Before you leave home, write the post office you will be sending mail to, to make sure they will hold your mail for your arrival. They are legally required to hold it *only* 10 days. Also find out what hours they are open. Finally, don't mail perishables.

Appendix C
Topographic Maps

The maps included in this book are all you'll need to safely walk the JMT. However, those interested in exploring off the trail, those planning to access/exit the trail at points other than its Happy Isles and Whitney Portal terminuses, and those who simply wish more detail will need other maps.

Wilderness Press updates and publishes four-color topographic maps (topos) on the handy 15′ scale once the standard for USGS topos. These maps, with a scale of about 1 inch = 1 mile, have been replaced by the 7$\frac{1}{2}$′ series, with a scale of nearly 2$\frac{3}{4}$ inches = 1 mile. The 7$\frac{1}{2}$′ topos provide more detail than the 15′ topos, but it takes four 7$\frac{1}{2}$′ maps to cover the area covered by one 15′ topo.

We think the Wilderness Press 15′ maps are simply the best ones for backpacking where they apply. The following Wilderness Press 15′ topos cover much, though not all, of the JMT and the routes to/from it:

Yosemite	Mt. Goddard
Tuolumne Meadows	Mt. Pinchot
Devils Postpile	Mt. Whitney
Mt. Abbot	

The following 7$\frac{1}{2}$′ maps cover the entire JMT. They are not fully up-to-date regarding the current JMT route; the maps in this book are better. Abbreviations like "Mtn." reflect the actual name used on the topo. Additional 7$\frac{1}{2}$′ maps needed to cover routes to/from the JMT are listed in Appendix B.

Half Dome	Bloody Mtn.	Split Mtn.
Merced Peak	Graveyard Peak	Mt. Pinchot
Tenaya Lake	Florence Lake	Mt. Clarence King
Vogelsang Peak	Mt. Hilgard	Mt. Williamson
Tioga Pass	Ward Mountain	Mt. Brewer
Koip Peak	Mt. Henry	Mt. Kaweah
Mt. Ritter	Mt. Darwin	Mt. Whitney
Mammoth Mtn.	Mt. Goddard	Mt. Langley
Crystal Crag	North Palisade	

Index

101

About this book's map numbers

Why are the map numbers in the "North to South" chapter of this book in reverse numerical order?

The maps were made for a previous edition of this book in which the main description of the John Muir Trail was south to north, which has always been the classic way to walk the trail. There was a much-abbreviated north-to-south description. Hence, the maps were numbered to support the main south-to-north description and indeed were embedded in that description.

Following the recommendations of many hikers for this latest edition, we gave equal weight to the north-to-south description, and we have put it first, because that is the direction in which most people now walk the John Muir Trail.

However, making all-new maps — as opposed to making the minor corrections necessary on the existing maps — would have been very expensive, adding to the cost of this book. We decided instead to correct and reuse the existing maps. After all, their numbers are going to be "backward" with respect to one or the other of the trail descriptions, and two sets of maps would be prohibitively expensive.

So, for the time being, we beg the forbearance of you north-to-south hikers. We hope in a future edition to provide new, north-to-south-oriented maps — and then we shall beg the forbearance of you south-to-north hikers!

——*Tom Winnett and Kathy Morey*